The Living Waters Series

Faith On Trial

The Startling Reality of Genuine Belief

The Living Waters Series

Faith On Trial
The Startling Reality of Genuine Belief

By

Lori Ann Moeszinger

THE RIDGE

PUBLISHING GROUP

The Ridge Publishing Group
Coeur d'Alene, Idaho, U.S.A.

Library of Congress Control Number: 2024918221

Faith On Trial: The Startling Reality of Genuine Belief / by Lori Ann
Moeszinger

ISBN: 978-1-956905-19-9 (e-book)

ISBN: 978-1-956905-18-2 (softcover)

1. Religion / Christian Living / General. 2. Religion / Christian Living /
Spiritual Growth. 3. Religion / Christian Life / Inspirational. 4. Religion /
Christian Life / Personal Growth. 5. Religion / Christian Living / Social
Issues. I. Title. II. Title Series

First Edition: September 2024

Printed in the United States of America

Contents

The Living Waters Series invites readers to rediscover the transformative power of faith. These books open the door to a renewed understanding of devotion, exploring the foundational truths of Christianity with fresh insights and heartfelt sincerity. Whether you are at the start of your spiritual journey or seeking to deepen your faith, these books offers guidance, inspiration, and a renewed sense of connection with Christ.

Join Our Community

Dive deeper into your faith and join a community of like-minded believers by connecting with us across multiple platforms:

- **Facebook Page**: Follow us at Guardians of Biblical Truth to stay updated with inspirational content and community discussions.
- **Facebook Group**: Join our closed group, Guardians of Biblical Truth Forum, for more personal interactions, where you can share, discuss, and grow in your understanding of biblical truths.
- **Blog**: Visit our blog at Jesus-Says.com for thoughtful posts, devotionals, and biblical interpretations aimed at nurturing your spiritual growth.
- **Social Media**: Connect with us on X and Instagram @NNSBible and Pinterest @GuardiansOfBiblicalTruth to get daily inspirations and engage with a community that values deep, scriptural truths.

We look forward to connecting with you and growing together in faith!

Faith On Trial

The Startling Reality of Genuine Belief

Introduction

What Does It Mean to Be a Real Christian?

Welcome to "Faith On Trial: The Startling Reality of Genuine Belief," the inaugural journey in The Living Waters Series. This book is more than a collection of thoughts and reflections on faith; it is an invitation to embark on a profound exploration of what it truly means to believe.

A Journey Into the Heart of Faith

At the core of this book lies a journey into the heart of faith. We live in a world where beliefs are often challenged, questioned, and scrutinized. "Faith On Trial" invites you to delve into these challenges, not with trepidation but with a spirit of exploration and discovery. It's an opportunity to confront the doubts, to understand the certainties, and to deepen your understanding of your faith.

Exploring the Realms of Belief and Doubt

In these pages, you will traverse the realms of belief and doubt, faith and assurance, and salvation and eternity. Each chapter is designed to guide you through the various facets of Christian faith, from the foundational principles to the more complex and often debated concepts. This exploration is not just as intellectual exercise; it's a journey of the heart and soul.

Engaging with Scripture and Personal Insight

Throughout "Faith On Trial," you will find a tapestry of scriptural insights, personal reflections, and theological explorations. The aim is to offer a balanced perspective that respects the depth of Scripture while acknowledging the personal nature of faith. Each chapter is crafted to provide both clarity and challenge, encouraging you to engage with the material in a way that is both thought-provoking and spiritually enriching.

For the Seeker and the Believer

Whether you are a seeker, new to the faith, or a long-standing believer, this book is for you. It is designed to meet you where you are in your spiritual journey. For the seeker, it offers a clear presentation of the Christian faith. For the believer, it provides a deeper dive into the complexities and joys of believing.

An Invitation to Journey Together

As you turn these pages, I invite you to journey with an open mind and a willing heart. Let the trials of faith become opportunities for growth. Let the questions lead to deeper understanding. And let the reality of genuine belief transform your life.

In "Faith On Trial," we begin a journey together through The Living Waters Series—a journey of discovery, challenge and transformation. Welcome aboard, and may this journey enlighten, encourage, and inspire you in your walk of faith.

Invitation

After reading this far, I thank you. With that said, I never start a book without giving an opportunity for people to get right with God. It is really inescapable, the fact that the Bible does teach eternity—once we are born, we live forever. There really is a heaven. There really is a hell. And the Bible tells us that we are going to spend eternity in one of these two places. The choice is ours. God has already made His choice. God loves us. He sent His only Son, Jesus Christ, to die on a cross for the forgiveness of our sins.

> "For God so loved the world, that He gave His only begotten Son, Jesus Christ, that whosoever believes in Him should not perish (die) but have everlasting life" (John 3:16).

Because God is holy, we need to be holy through Jesus Christ; He will never change, He is immutable, unchangeable. He is in the total state of sinless perfection in everything that He does. But you and I are not holy. By nature, we are sinful and selfish. And because we are sinful and selfish, we are separated from a holy God. But God told us, we were created in His image, and it is His desire to redeem us to right relationship with Him. Therefore, Jesus is the bridge between the holiness of God and the unholiness of humanity. And the Bible also tells us that the only way to break the curse of sin and to find right relationship with God is through Jesus Christ.

"Jesus says unto him, I am the way, the truth, and the life: no man comes unto the Father, but by Me" (John 14:6).

The Gospel

The word "gospel" in the Greek original text means "good news of the kingdom of God." In Christianity, the term "good news" refers to the story of Jesus Christ's birth, ministry, death, and resurrection. Jesus Christ, the Son of God, died for our sins and rose again, eternally triumphant over His enemies—so that there is now no condemnation for those who believe but only everlasting joy. Wherefore the fullness of the gospel is in God Himself—enjoyed by His redeemed people.

Through the death, the ministry, the burial, and the resurrection of Jesus Christ, you and I not only have power over sin, but we have power over sickness, disease, and infirmity—yesterday, today, and forever. The same seven ways

Jesus healed in the New Testament are still available to every believer today. Jesus Christ is still the great physician, and no weapon formed against His children shall prosper in the name of the Lord Jesus Christ.

> "But He was wounded for our transgressions (sins),
> He was bruised for our iniquities (immoral behavior):
> the chastisement (punishment) of our peace was
> upon Him; and with His stripes (the marks on His
> back from His beating) we are healed" (Isaiah 53:5).

> "Who His own self bore our sins in His own body on
> the tree (cross), that we being dead to sins, should live
> unto righteousness: by whose stripes you are healed"
> (1 Peter 2:24).

Making Peace with God

How do you make peace with God?

You have to do two things:

First, you must believe in the gospel—the teaching and revelation of Christ. The gospel, just as the Scripture says: (1) Jesus Christ, God the Father's only Son, lived on this Earth, (2) died on a cross for the forgiveness of our sins, (3) was buried, (4) was raised from the dead on the third day, (5) stayed on this Earth for 40 days before ascending to heaven, (6) promised to return, and (7) we are saved by faith alone in Christ alone—this is called the doctrine of salvation.

Second, you must receive Christ by doing three things: (1) Recognize and admit your sins. The Bible says, "For all have sinned, and come short of the glory of God" (Romans 3:23). (2) Repent of your sins. Jesus said, "No, I tell you; but unless you repent, you will all likewise perish (die)" (Luke 13:3). Repentance means you recognize your sins; you admit your life is headed in the wrong direction, and now you must be willing to turn your back on sin and turn your heart to Christ. (3) Receive Jesus Christ as your personal Lord and Savior. Commit your heart to Him by faith—in childlike faith; showing the good qualities that children have, such as trusting people, being honest and enthusiastic, expressing a childlike innocence or quality.

> "The Lord is not slack concerning His promise, as some men count slackness; but is longsuffering toward us, not willing that any should perish (die), but that all should come to repentance" (2 Peter 3:9).

That word "men" in the Greek is generic; it means "men and women." Therefore, if you have never recognized and repented of your sins (changed your carnal ways). If you've never had a relationship with God. Or perhaps, you are backslidden or away from God or you've wandered. The Bible says, "I will heal your backsliding, I will love them freely: for My anger is turned away from him" (Hosea 14:4). You can come home to your heavenly Father today, and He will love you, and forgive you, and cleanse you, and strengthen you to be what He's called you to be.

It isn't by accident that you are reading this book. I believe the Lord by His leading and His mercy brought us together. And so, I want to ask you to pray the prayer of salvation—also called the prayer of faith and sometimes called the sinner's prayer—to make peace with God. Just, with a sincere heart, pray the prayer of salvation out loud in childlike faith and make a commitment right now.

Why out loud? Because Christ did everything publicly.

"For whosoever shall be ashamed of Me and of My words, of him shall the Son of Man be ashamed, when He comes in the glory of His Father with His holy angels" (Luke 9:26; also in Mark 8:38).

And after you've done that, go to our Publisher Website at https://www.RidgePublishingGroup.com, and click on "Subscribe" to receive our monthly **Guardians of Biblical Truth New Beginnings Newsletter** sent directly to your inbox. Also, on our website, you will find the prequel to this book, Passion for Christ: New Beginnings, available for free in PDF format when you subscribe. The e-book and print book versions are both available for purchase at Amazon.com and other retailers. Follow us on our Amazon Author Central page and learn more about next steps in your walk with God as we upload more Bible-based books. Why? Because this isn't the end of what God's going to do in your life, just the beginning.

"Go therefore and make disciples of all nations, baptizing them in the name of the Father and of the Son and of the Holy Spirit, teaching them to observe all that I have commanded you. And behold, I am with you always, to the end of the age" (Matthew 28:19-20).

With a sincere heart, just pray this, out loud:

"Heavenly Father, today as I was reading the Bible, you were speaking to me. I want to be right with God. I recognize my sins and I ask for forgiveness. I believe Jesus Christ is your Son. I believe that He died on the cross as payment for sin and rose again as the hope of the world. And I recognize that Jesus is the only salvation and the only Savior available.

In childlike faith, I trust in the Lord Jesus from this day forward. I repent of my sins, and I trust in the blood that was shed on the cross for the forgiveness of my sins. Cleanse me; my mind, my body, and my spirit. Come into my heart. And I vow this day, I will live for you all the days of my life. Guide my life and help me to do your will. Fill me with the Holy Spirit and give me the power to be what you want me to be. Be my Lord and Savior.

According to the Bible which cannot lie, all who call upon the name of the Lord, shall be saved. Today, I'm saved. I'm forgiven. I'm delivered. I'm healed. The curse of sin and sickness and lack in my life are now broken. And I have become the righteousness of God through Jesus Christ. And I'll never be the same. I pray this in Jesus Christ's precious name. Amen."

The Bible said either your Father is God, or your father is the devil. And the Bible said that the power of sin and Satan comes to steal, and to kill, and to destroy. But Jesus said:

"The thief comes not, but for to steal, and to kill, and to destroy; I come that they might have life, and that they might have it more abundantly" (John 10:10).

INTRODUCTION

Jesus is the master of life. And if you want to walk in the life of forgiveness and have that relationship with God the Father, you can begin that today. All you have to do is pray the prayer of salvation to make peace with God—in doing so, you become a born again Christian.

> "Therefore if any man be in Christ, he is a new creature: old things are passed away; behold, all things become new" (2 Corinthians 5:17).

"Total Surrender: My Story and Your Blueprint for a Meaningful Life" is not just an autobiography about my call with God. It is a clarion call (a call to something that is hard to ignore). It is a wakeup call to all of humanity to choose God before it's too late; and get prepared for the second coming of Jesus Christ, our Lord and Savior—time is near, He is knocking at the door:

> "Behold, I stand at the door and knock. If anyone hears My voice and opens the door, I will come in to him and eat with him, and he with Me" (Revelation 3:20).

When you know God and understand the wisdom of the Bible, it will change you! This is our calling—our true purpose in life. Let the Lord into your life; He has a plan . . . when you do that, amazing things start to happen: You'll become passionate about God. You'll begin to crave to think and speak in line with Jesus' ways. You'll start to see yourself the way Christ sees you. You'll habitually tune into the Holy Spirit, who lives within those in Christ, to check for a sense of peace in your choices. And then miracles begin to happen . . .

CHAPTER ONE

The Awakening: Understanding Genuine Faith and False Assurance

"Count it all joy, my brothers, when you meet trials of various kinds, for you know that the testing of your faith produces steadfastness. And let steadfastness have its full effect, that you may be perfect and complete, lacking in nothing." —JAMES 1:2–4 ESV

In a world bustling with myriad beliefs and ideologies, where every step is a dance with doubt and conviction, we embark on a journey to understand the essence of genuine faith. This journey is not merely an academic excursion but a deep dive into the soul of what it means to believe, to hope, and to trust.

Welcome to "The Awakening," a chapter that seeks to unravel the intricate tapestry of faith and assurance. Here, we don't just skim the surface of belief; we plunge into its depths, exploring its nuances, challenges, and the profound impact it has on our lives.

As you turn these pages, you will encounter the multifaceted nature of faith. We will explore why faith, a concept as old as humanity itself, remains a cornerstone of our existence. We will delve into the often-misunderstood dichotomy between genuine faith and false assurance, shining a light on the subtle yet crucial differences that define them.

This chapter is a call to introspection and understanding. It's an invitation to question, to seek, and to discover. It's a journey that will take us through the heart of what it means to choose faith, to test its authenticity, to grapple with doubts, and ultimately, to find assurance in our beliefs.

Whether you are a seeker, a skeptic, or a believer, this chapter aims to offer a space for reflection and understanding. Here, we recognize that faith is not a one-size-fits-all concept but a personal journey unique to each individual.

So, let us embark on this exploration with open hearts and minds. Let us journey together through "The Awakening," as we uncover the startling reality of genuine belief and the peace that comes with true assurance.

Life's Most Important Choice

In the quiet stillness of a world that never sleeps, there lies a profound question, echoing through the chambers of every human heart: What do I truly believe?

This is not a query about fleeting thoughts or temporary convictions. It is the deep, pulsating inquiry about the essence of our being, the very core of our existence. For at the heart of every life decision, every joy and sorrow, every hope and fear, is the matter of belief. Not just any belief, but genuine, unshakable faith.

As we embark on this journey, let's first dispel a common misconception: faith is not a mere acceptance of doctrines or a passive agreement with religious teachings. No, genuine faith is a vibrant, living force. It's a dynamic choice that shapes our actions, molds our character, and defines our destiny.

But here's the starting reality: amidst the ocean of beliefs, there exists a subtle yet significant distinction between genuine faith and false assurance. This section seeks to illuminate that difference, guiding you through an awakening to understand the nature of true belief.

Consider for a moment the world around us, teeming with various forms of faith. There are those who adhere strictly to religious texts, and others who find their faith in the wonders of science. Some place their belief in ideologies, while others in the intrinsic goodness of humanity. Yet, amidst this diversity, a crucial question arises: is faith genuine, or is it merely a facade of assurance, a shield against the uncertainties of life?

To unravel this mystery, we must delve into the core of what makes faith genuine. Genuine faith is not just a comfort in times of distress; it's a compass that guides us through the storms of life. It's not a blind leap into the abyss, but a reasoned, conscious choice grounded in our deepest values and truths.

The journey to understanding genuine faith begins with introspection. It's a path that requires us to confront our fears, our doubts and our prejudices. It asks us to examine the foundations of our beliefs, to question the unquestioned, and to seek the truth with an open heart and mind.

As we explore this path, we'll encounter stories of individuals who faced life's most significant choice: to cling to the false assurance of unexamined beliefs or to embrace the awakening of genuine faith. Their experiences, fraught with challenges and triumphs, offer profound insights into the nature of true belief.

So, let us embark on this journey together, with open minds and willing hearts. Let us explore the depths of genuine faith and distinguish it from the shallow waters of false assurance. For in the exploration lies life's most important choice, a choice that shapes our destiny and defines the essence of our being.

―――――――

Emily's Journey to Life's Most Crucial Choice

Emily, a 34-year-old community organizer with an inviting smile and a persistent frown of concentration, often found herself pacing late at night in her modestly furnished apartment, overwhelmed by the weight of existential questions. Her personal attire, usually a mix of professional and casual, subtly displayed a silver necklace with a small, intricate compass pendant—a gift from her grandmother and a symbol of guidance.

Emily's nights were restless, haunted by a single gnawing question: "What do I truly believe?" This wasn't about fleeting doubts or superficial queries; it was about the foundation of her very existence. The ambiguity of her faith kept her awake, yearning for something genuine to hold onto—a beacon that could provide real direction in her earnest quest for truth.

The transformative moment came unexpectedly during a community workshop she organized, themed "Navigating Belief: Understanding Our True North." As various speakers shared their journeys of faith, from staunch atheism to devout spirituality, Emily experienced a profound internal shift. The testimony of an elderly woman, who spoke of finding genuine faith not just as comfort but as a guiding principle in life, struck a chord within her. It was in this moment, amidst the attentive silence of the room, that Emily felt a surge of clarity wash over her, as if the pieces of her fragmented beliefs were finally aligning.

The community hall, with its high ceilings and echo of attentive whispers, was dimly lit except for the spotlight on the speakers, creating an atmosphere of reverence and introspection. The scent of brewed coffee lingered, blending with the subtle fragrance of aged wood from the surrounding walls. As Emily listened, her fingers absentmindedly traced the contours of her compass pendant, grounding her in the moment.

As the workshop concluded, Emily's newfound understanding compelled her to approach the elderly speaker. With a voice steadier than she felt, Emily expressed her gratitude and shared her fears of embracing a path of genuine faith. The reassuring grip of the speaker's hand on hers, warm and affirming, felt like a passing of torch—of faith and conviction.

In the weeks that followed, Emily's life began to reflect her inner change. Her decisions, once marred by doubt, were now guided by a confident understanding of her beliefs. She started to volunteer more, driven by a clear sense of purpose and a commitment to make a meaningful impact, resonating with her true beliefs.

This chapter in Emily's life was not just about finding faith; it was about discovering her true self and extending that authenticity to her community. Her story illustrates the profound impact of confronting and embracing one's beliefs, offering a powerful testament to the transformative potential of genuine faith. As readers witness Emily's journey, they too are invited to examine the depths of their own beliefs, to distinguish between mere comfort and true guidance, making life's most crucial choice: to live with genuine faith.

Four Ways/Tests to See if Your Faith is Really Genuine

After peeling back the layers of what constitutes genuine faith, we now stand at a crossroad. How do we discern the authenticity of our belief? Is there a way to test the genuineness of our faith? Indeed, there are paths to explore and tests to undertake. Here, we delve into four profound ways to examine the authenticity of your faith.

Test 1: The Test of Values—What Guides Your Decisions?

At the heart of genuine faith lies a compass of values that guides your decisions. This is the first test. Ask yourself: What are the principles that guide my life? Are my choices a reflection of a deep-seated belief, or are they swayed by convenience and external pressures? Genuine faith is not swayed by the changing tides of societal norms or personal gain. It is constant, guiding you to act with integrity, even when it's challenging.

Test 2: The Test of Adversity—Does Your Faith Withstand the Storms?

The second test is found in the crucible of adversity. It's easy to hold onto beliefs when the seas are calm, but the true test of faith is how it holds up in the storm. Reflect on the moments of a trial in your life. Did your faith provide a steadfast anchor, or did it waver under pressure? Genuine faith acts as a resilient pillar, offering strength and hope in the face of challenges.

Test 3: The Test of Growth—Does Your Faith Propel You Forward?

Genuine faith is not static. It propels growth, both personal and spiritual. This is the third test. Examine whether your faith has been a catalyst for positive change and development. Has it challenged you to grow, to expand your understanding, and to embrace empathy and love more fully? Genuine faith encourages evolution, not just to the self, but of the ideas and understanding we hold.

Test 4: The Test of Connection—Does Your Faith Foster Community and Compassion?

Finally, the fourth test looks beyond the individual to the community. Genuine faith doesn't isolate; it connects. It fosters a sense of unity, compassion, and a commitment to the welfare of others. Consider how your faith impacts your relationships and your view of the world. Does it lead you to act with kindness, to seek understanding, and to bridge divides? Genuine faith sees the interconnectedness of all life and inspires actions that uphold this principle.

These four tests offer a mirror to reflect upon the nature of your faith. They are not meant to judge, but to enlighten and guide towards deeper understanding and authenticity. As we navigate through these tests, we uncover layers of our belief, revealing the true essence of our faith. This is the awakening— a journey towards understanding the startling reality of genuine belief.

Ryan's Architectural Journey in Faith

Ryan, a 42-year-old architect known for his meticulous designs and thoughtful approach to every project, finds himself facing a different kind of blueprint: his spiritual life. He's a man of medium build with a thoughtful gaze that often lingers on the horizon as if looking for answers. Always dressed in his trademark crisp, blue button-down shirt, he carries the aura of someone constantly in search of deeper meaning. Recently, Ryan has felt a growing unease, a sense that his spiritual foundation might not be as solid as the structures he creates.

Lying awake at night, the quiet of his room amplifies his inner turmoil. The silence isn't peaceful; it's heavy with doubts about the authenticity of his faith. "Is my belief true enough? Strong enough? Real enough?" These questions haunt him, echoing through his mind with an intensity that rivals his most stressful days at the office.

During a Sunday service, as he listens to a sermon on the "Tests of Genuine Faith," Ryan experiences a pivotal moment. The preacher talks about the 'Test of Adversity'—how true faith is not just about weathering storms but finding direction through them. At that moment, Ryan recalls the toughest times of his life: his divorce, his father's illness. He realizes that during those times, instead of feeling abandoned, he felt a guiding hand, a comfort that he hadn't fully acknowledged until now.

The church is filled with the soft hum of a congregation in deep contemplation, the wooden pews carrying the weight of shared human experiences. The scent of polished wood and the faint floral aroma from the day's bouquets fill the air, grounding Ryan in the moment. As he sits there, his fingers trace the grain of the wood in the pew in front of him, connecting the physical touch to the spiritual truth being revealed.

This revelation marks a profound change in Ryan. He begins to see his past trials not as moments of divine absence, but as periods of silent teaching and subtle guidance. He realizes that his faith, though quiet, has been a constant companion, subtly shaping his decisions and providing unseen support.

Inspired by this new understanding, Ryan starts to approach his spiritual doubts like he would a complex architectural problem—to be examined, understood, and integrated into a stronger whole. He engages more actively in community service, applying his skills to help build homes for those in need, seeing this as a practical application of his faith and a way to test its strength and resilience.

In sharing his journey, Ryan becomes a beacon for others wrestling with similar doubts. His story, a testimony to the power of understanding and embracing the true nature of one's faith, offers a blueprint for others to examine and reinforce their own beliefs. Through his experience, readers are invited to reflect on the authenticity of their faith, encouraging them to build and fortify their spiritual foundations with as much care as Ryan applies to his architectural creations.

5 Reasons Why People Doubt Their Salvation

Doubt, like a shadow, often walks hand-in-hand with faith. It's a universal experience, one that can either shake the foundations of our beliefs or strengthen them. Understanding why we doubt can be a powerful step in solidifying our faith. Let's explore five common reasons why people might doubt their salvation, their place in the divine tapestry of belief and existence.

Reason 1: The Expectation of Perfection—When We Fall Short

One of the most pervasive reasons for doubt is the expectation of perfection. Many of us grow up with the notion that faith, once found, renders us immune to failure or sin. However, this is a misconception. We are all works in progress, navigating through our imperfections. When we inevitably fall short of our own or others' expectations, doubt creeps in, whispering that perhaps we are not truly saved. It's crucial to remember that faith is a journey, not a destination.

Reason 2: Misunderstanding Grace—Believing We Must Earn Salvation

Closely linked to the first, the second reason lies in misunderstanding grace. In a world that often emphasizes earning and deserving, it's easy to mistakenly apply these concepts to salvation. This belief can lead to doubt when we feel we haven't done enough to 'earn' our salvation. Genuine faith understands that salvation is not a prize for good deeds but a gift of grace, unearned and freely given.

Reason 3: The Silence of God—When Heaven Seems Silent

At times, in the depths of prayer or despair, heaven seems silent. This perceived silence can be mistaken as abandonment or a sign of unsaved status. Yet, this silence is often not a lack of response but an invitation to deeper trust and understanding. In these moments of silence, faith is both tested and fortified.

Reason 4: Comparing Faith Journeys—The Illusion of Others' Perfection

Another common source of doubt is the comparison of our faith journey with others'. In our interconnected world, it's easy to look at others' lives and feel that their faith is somehow more valid, more vibrant, or more genuine. This comparison overlooks the unique, personal nature of faith and salvation. Everyone's journey is different, and doubt often arises when we forget this truth.

Reason 5: Life's Hardships and Disappointments—When Faith Doesn't Align with Reality

Finally, doubt can stem from the harsh realities of life. When faced with pain, suffering, or injustice. It's natural to question why things happen if we are saved or beloved by God. These moments of hardship challenge us to find a deeper, more resilient understanding of our faith, one that can encompass and transcend life's complexities.

These five reasons for doubt are not just challenges; they are opportunities for growth and deeper understanding. By recognizing and exploring these doubts, we can move towards a more secure and profound faith. This exploration is part of the awakening, part of understanding the startling reality of genuine belief.

===

Harper's Journey Through Doubt and Discovery

Harper, a 35-year-old community organizer, always wears her trusty silver locket—a gift from her grandmother that symbolizes her deep-rooted faith. Known for her compassionate nature and the earnestness with which she approaches her work, Harper has recently found herself grappling with shadows of doubt about her salvation, especially during the quieter moments of her bustling life.

Every evening, as Harper sits on her small balcony overlooking the busy street below, her thoughts turn introspective. The city lights blur into a cascade of colors, mirroring the turmoil inside her—doubts about whether her faith measures up, whether her flaws and failures have distanced her from salvation. These thoughts whisper with growing insistence, challenging the assurance she once felt in her spiritual journey.

One late autumn evening, while organizing a local food drive, Harper encounters a homeless man whose profound gratitude for a simple meal strikes a deep chord within her. In his eyes, she sees not judgment but a reflection of genuine human struggle and resilience. This pivotal moment jolts her, stirring a realization about the true nature of grace and salvation.

The air is crisp, and the scent of autumn leaves mingles with the city's exhaust. Harper hands out warm meals, her breath visible in the chilly air, her hands slightly trembling—not from the cold, but from a burgeoning revelation. The grateful smile of the homeless man, his weather-beaten hands clasping the food, becomes a profound testament to her wavering faith.

This encounter illuminates Harper's misconceptions about grace—realizing it's not about earning salvation through flawless faith, but accepting it as a gift, despite imperfections. She understands now that her doubts don't signify a lack of salvation but are part of her spiritual growth, challenging her to deepen her understanding and reliance on grace.

Emboldened by this new understanding, Harper begins to approach her community work with a renewed vigor and a deeper sense of purpose. She sees each act of kindness not as a step toward earning salvation but as an expression of the grace she's already received. Sharing her story with others, Harper becomes a beacon of hope, showing that doubt can be a catalyst for stronger, more resilient faith.

In her narrative, Harper's journey resonates with many who battle similar doubts. Her story is a vivid illustration that faith is not measured by the absence of doubt but by the actions we take and the grace we embrace amidst those doubts. Through her experiences, others find the courage to examine their beliefs, embrace their imperfections, and accept the unearned gift of salvation with open hearts.

How Can I Be Sure of My Salvation

The quest for certainty in our salvation is a deeply human one, born out of a longing for security and a sense of belonging in the grand scheme of things. This longing often leads us to ask: How can I be sure of my salvation? Let's explore this profound question and uncover the pathways that lead to assurance.

Embracing the Promise of Faith

The first step towards assurance is embracing the promise of faith. This isn't about blind acceptance, but a conscious decision to trust in the principles and truths that your faith teaches. It's about believing in the promises made by your faith system—whether it's the assurance of love, redemption, forgiveness, or eternal life. The key here is not just intellectual acceptance but a deep, heartfelt trust.

Reflecting on Personal Experiences of Grace

Take a moment to reflect on your personal experiences of grace and transformation. These moments, whether big or small, serve as landmarks of your spiritual journey. Remember the times when you felt a profound sense of peace, an unexpected forgiveness, or a moment of clarity. These experiences are personal affirmations of your connection with the divine, reinforcing the assurance of your salvation.

The Role of Community in Affirming Faith

Faith is often strengthened and affirmed within a community. Engaging with a community of believers provides support, understanding, and a shared journey. Witnessing the faith of others and experiencing their support can reinforce your own beliefs and offer a sense of solidarity. Communities also provide a space for dialogue, where doubts can be expressed and explored in a supportive environment.

Continual Growth and Learning

Assurance in salvation is also found through continual growth and learning. Engaging with religious texts, spiritual practices, and ongoing self-reflection deepens understanding and strengthens faith. This process of learning isn't just about acquiring knowledge; it's about allowing your beliefs to evolve and mature, which in turn fortifies the assurance of your faith.

Testing Faith Against Life's Challenges

Finally, consider how your faith stands against the challenges of life. True faith is not just for moments of tranquility but also for times of turmoil. When your faith provides comfort, guidance, and resilience in the face of life's trials, it reaffirms its authenticity and your assurance in it.

In the quest to be sure of our salvation, we find that the journey itself is revelatory. It's a path that involves trust, reflection, community, learning, and resilience. This journey is integral to the awakening, to understanding the nature of genuine faith and the assurance that comes with it.

———————

Noah's Quest for Faith and Assurance

Noah, a 42-year-old teacher, known for his reflective nature and deep thoughtfulness, often sports a well-worn leather journal where he pens his thoughts and struggles with faith. Recently, his entries have focused on his search for assurance in his salvation—a quest intensified by the recent loss of his father, a devout man who was Noah's spiritual anchor.

As the school year winds down, Noah finds himself at a crossroads, his heart heavy with doubt. His father's passing not only left a void in his life but also in his spiritual confidence. Each night, as he sits under the old oak tree in his backyard—their favorite spot for deep conversations—he wrestles with a longing for the same unshakeable faith his father possessed.

During a routine school day, while teaching a lesson on historical faith figures known for their spiritual crises, a student asks Noah, "How do you know if you're truly saved?" This question, simple yet profound, hits Noah unexpectedly, resonating with his own uncertainties. It serves as a catalyst, compelling him to explore the depth of his beliefs.

The classroom is alive with the buzz of engaged teenagers, the walls adorned with posters of historical and philosophical figures. As Noah faces the eager, expectant faces of his students, the afternoon sunlight streams through the window, casting a warm glow that reminds him of his father's comforting presence.

Motivated by his student's inquiry, Noah decides to initiate a weekly discussion group, inviting students and faculty alike to explore their beliefs and doubts openly. This community becomes a crucible for Noah's transformation. Through shared stories and diverse perspectives, he begins to see his personal experiences of grace—the subtle yet profound moments of peace and insight he's encountered throughout his life.

Through this community, Noah re-engages with his faith not just as a set of doctrines, but as a living, breathing journey. He revisits his father's teachings, realizing that his doubts do not diminish his faith but deepen it. Each discussion, each shared doubt, and affirmation, weaves into a tapestry of stronger belief. Noah's journal entries begin to change, reflecting a renewed confidence in his salvation, rooted in a vibrant, evolving faith.

This story of Noah illustrates that assurance in salvation often comes through the community, reflection, and embracing faith as a dynamic journey. It highlights that doubt, when approached with curiosity and openness, can lead to deeper understanding and stronger conviction. Noah's journey offers hope and guidance to those wrestling with similar doubts, proving that the path to assurance is as much about the questions we ask as the answers we find.

Conclusion

As we draw the curtains on this opening chapter, "The Awakening," we pause to reflect on the profound journey we've embarked upon. Together, we have navigated the intricate landscape of genuine faith, waded through the murky waters of false assurance, and stood face to face with the true essence of belief.

This chapter has not just been an exploration of concepts; it has been a voyage into the depths of our spiritual consciousness. We began by unveiling the multifaceted nature of genuine faith and false assurance, dissecting the nuanced differences that define them. We then delved into the tests and signs of authentic faith, offering tools for introspection and self-discovery.

Our journey took us through the reasons why doubts about salvation surface, inviting us to embrace our uncertainties as part of our faith journey. We concluded by addressing the perennial question of assurance in salvation, discovering that certainty in faith is as much about the journey as it is about the destination.

One of the key takeaways from this chapter is the power of introspection. The journey towards understanding genuine faith is deeply personal and requires us to look inward, to question, and to seek. It is a journey that does not shy away from doubts but embraces them as essential components of a vibrant and living faith.

As we conclude this chapter, let us carry forward the insights, reflections, and questions that have arisen. This is not the end of our exploration but merely the beginning. Each topic we have touched upon opens doors to deeper understanding and further inquiry.

I invite you to continue this journey with an open heart and a curious mind. The path of faith is not linear; it is a winding road filled with discoveries, challenges, and transformations. Let the awakening we have experienced in this chapter be a catalyst for ongoing exploration and growth in your spiritual journey. And may this awakening of your understanding be as enriching as it is enlightening, guiding you towards a deep, more authentic experience of your faith.

CHAPTER TWO

The Crossroads of Belief: Exploring Salvation's Terrifying Truths

"Now faith is the assurance of things hoped for, the conviction of things not seen." —HEBREWS 1:1 ESV

As we venture deeper into the exploration of faith, we arrive at chapter two: "The Crossroads of Belief," a chapter that beckons us to confront the more daunting aspects of our spiritual journey. Here, we stand at the intersection of comfort and challenge, tradition and transformation, exploring the truths about salvation that can be as unsettling as they are enlightening.

In this chapter, we delve into the enigmatic and often intimidating realms of prophecy, divine justice, and the ultimate fate of humanity. We grapple with questions that have echoed through the corridors of time and across the expanse of human consciousness. These are the questions that stir the soul and challenge the mind, compelling us to look beyond the surface of our beliefs and confront the realities that lie beneath.

We begin with an exploration of what is considered the most terrifying prophecy passage in the Bible, a scripture that has captivated and confounded believers for centuries. This exploration is not meant to instill fear, but to invite introspection and understanding of the profound messages encapsulated within these prophetic words.

From there, we journey into the heart of a question as old as belief itself: Do all roads lead to heaven? This inquiry challenges us to consider the diversity of faiths and the nature of salvation, pushing us to think critically about the inclusivity and exclusivity of our spiritual paths.

We then turn to the pivotal distinction between religion and relationships, exploring how our connection with the divine transcends rituals and doctrines to become a deeply personal experience. This part of the journey examines how structured faith intersects with personal spirituality, and how each can enrich and inform the other.

"The Crossroads of Belief" is more than a chapter; it's a journey into the depths of what it means to believe, to question, and to seek truth. It's a passage through the challenging terrains of faith, where we confront the terrifying truths and the profound mysteries of salvation.

As we embark on this journey, let us do so with open hearts and minds, ready to explore, question, and grow. Let us embrace the uncertainty and the beauty of the journey, for it is in seeking that we find, and in questioning that we come closer to the essence of our faith.

Welcome to "The Crossroads of Belief." Welcome to a journey of discovery, challenge, and deeper understanding.

The Most Terrifying Prophecy Passage in the Bible

In the vast expanse of scriptural narratives, filled with stories of hope, redemption, and divine mysteries, there lies a passage of prophecy so profound and unsettling that it has echoed through the ages, challenging the hearts and minds of believers. This passage, often regarded as the most terrifying in the Bible, compels us to confront the depths of our faith and the realities of salvation.

As we tread into this section, we stand at a crossroads of belief, where light meets shadow, and assurance grapples with apprehension. Here, we delve into the complexities of a prophecy that has both confounded and captivated scholars, theologians, and seekers alike.

This passage, shrouded in metaphor and steeped in apocalyptic imagery, paints a picture of a future where the very foundations of faith are shaken. It speaks of trials and tribulations, of a time when the essence of what we hold true is tested against the unrelenting forces of change and challenge.

But why, you might ask, focus on a prophecy so unsettling? The answer lies in the heart of what it means to genuinely engage with our beliefs. To truly understand faith, we must be willing to explore even its most daunting aspects. We must be brave enough to ask difficult questions and seek truths that may be uncomfortable.

The exploration of this terrifying prophecy is not just an exercise in theological study; it's a journey into the soul of belief itself. It asks us to examine the strength and authenticity of our faith. It challenges us to consider how we would stand in the face of profound spiritual upheaval.

In this chapter, we will unpack this prophecy, exploring its historical context, its theological implications, and its relevance to our contemporary world. We will grapple with the questions it raises about divine justice, human suffering, and the nature of redemption.

But more than anything, this exploration is an invitation to deeper understanding and reflection. It's an opportunity to look beyond the surface of our beliefs and confront the realities that shape our spiritual journey.

So, as we venture into this chapter, let us do so with open minds and courageous hearts. Let us explore these terrifying truths not with fear, but with a desire to deepen our understanding of the divine narrative and place within it. And so, welcome to a journey through the most terrifying prophecy passage in the Bible.

Evelyn's Journey Through Prophecy and Faith

Evelyn, a 35-year-old community leader and mother of two, has always been the pillar of strength in her neighborhood. Known for her calm demeanor and insightful wisdom, Evelyn wears a simple silver cross necklace—a gift from her grandmother and a symbol of her deep-rooted faith. Recently, she's been haunted by the vivid images and unsettling messages from a particularly daunting prophecy passage she encountered during a Bible study.

One stormy evening, as lightning flashes across the sky, mirroring the turmoil in her heart, Evelyn sits in her quiet study room, her Bible open to the troubling prophecy. The shadows cast by the candlelight make the words seem to dance menacingly on the pages. She wrestles with a growing fear, not just for her own faith but for her children's future. How could such terrifying events possibly unfold? How could she prepare her family and her community for such challenging times?

As the thunder rolls, a sudden realization strikes Evelyn as forcefully as the lightning outside her window. This prophecy, though terrifying, is not just a warning but a call to deeper faith and action. She recalls her grandmother's words, "Faith is not just about enduring calm seas but also about braving the storms."

Determined to turn her fear into action, Evelyn organizes a community meeting at the local community hall—a cozy, well-worn building that has seen many gatherings. The room is filled with familiar faces, young and old, all seeking understanding and comfort.

With the storm raging outside, Evelyn shares her insights into the prophecy. She speaks not only of the terrifying events foretold but also of the resilience and redemption that can come from such trials. Her voice, firm yet comforting, reassures the community that while the prophecy speaks of testing times, it also calls for unity, courage, and hope.

Evelyn's interpretation of the prophecy transforms the community's fear into a collective resolve. They decide to strengthen their faith together, establishing support groups and educational programs to delve deeper into their beliefs and prepare spiritually for any future adversities. Evelyn's leadership and the silver cross around her neck shine as beacons of hope and strength.

This story of Evelyn illustrates how confronting terrifying truths within our faith can catalyze a deeper communal understanding and proactive spiritual readiness. It shows that the value of engaging with daunting prophecies lies not in succumbing to fear but in harnessing it to fortify faith and foster a supportive community.

Do All Roads Lead to Heaven?

In our journey through the terrains of faith and belief, we arrive at a question as ancient as it is provocative: Do all roads lead to heaven? This inquiry is not just a theological puzzle to be solved; it's profound exploration of the diversity of beliefs and the nature of salvation.

As we navigate this topic, we tread on a path lined with myriad beliefs and doctrines, each proclaiming its own truth and path to the divine. The question beckons us to consider the vast tapestry of religious experiences and convictions that make up our world. It challenges us to ponder the essence of divine justice and mercy.

The Diversity of Belief Systems

First, let's acknowledge the incredible diversity of belief systems that exist around us. From the ancient rituals of indigenous faiths to the structured doctrines of major world religions, the variety is staggering. Each tradition offers its own understanding of salvation, its own roadmap to the divine. How do these diverse paths intersect with the idea that there might be one true way to heaven?

The Nature of Truth and Salvation

This question also invites us to reflect on the nature of truth and salvation. Is truth exclusive or inclusive? Does salvation belong to a select few who follow a prescribed path, or is it available to all, regardless of the route taken? These are not just philosophical musings but deeply personal inquiries that touch the core of our faith.

The Role of Faith and Deeds

Another dimension to consider is the role of faith and deeds in the journey to heaven. How do different belief systems weigh the importance of faith versus actions? Some traditions emphasize a faith-centered path to salvation, while others focus on the deeds and actions of individuals. Exploring this aspect sheds light on the diverse understandings of what it takes to reach the divine.

Seeking Understanding in a Pluralistic World

In our modern, pluralistic world, the question of whether all roads lead to heaven is more relevant than ever. It challenges us to seek understanding and empathy in a world brimming with diverse beliefs. It invites us to engage in dialogue, to listen and learn from others, and to reflect on our own beliefs with humility and openness.

As we ponder whether all roads lead to heaven, we are not merely seeking an answer but engaging in a journey of understanding. This exploration is a crucial part of the crossroads of belief, where we confront the realities of salvation and the vastness of human faith. Let us continue this journey with open hearts and minds, embracing the complexities and seeking deeper truths.

Oliver's Architectural Pathways to Unity

Oliver, a seasoned architect, aged 48, known for his dedication to building bridges that connect disparate communities across ravines and rivers, symbolizes more than just structural achievements. He wears a well-worn leather bracelet, inscribed with symbols from various world religions, a testament to his deep respect for diverse beliefs. His life's work, influenced by his profound spiritual journey and encounters with different faiths, mirrors his inner quest for understanding the paths that lead to heaven.

Oliver has always been driven by a deep-seated curiosity about the world and its myriad cultures and religions. This curiosity is coupled with a heartfelt desire to find inclusivity in spirituality. He often lies awake at night, pondering over the architectural blueprints spread across his table, which symbolically represent the intricate pathways of faith leading to salvation.

During a multicultural religious conference, where Oliver is invited to speak about his architectural projects that facilitate physical and metaphorical connections, he experiences a profound moment of clarity. As he listens to leaders from various faiths discuss the concept of heaven and salvation, Oliver sees a parallel between his bridges and the theological question at hand—do all roads lead to heaven?

In his speech, Oliver shares a story about a bridge he once designed, which connected two historically conflicting communities. He draws a parallel to this with the idea of spiritual pathways, emphasizing that while the destinations might be envisaged differently, the essence of seeking a higher ground, or heaven, is fundamentally similar across cultures.

Oliver proposes a concept called 'The Bridge of Beliefs'— a symbolic and physical space where people of different faiths can come together to share, learn, and understand each other's paths. His vision is met with enthusiastic applause and interest, sparking a movement towards a more interconnected spiritual dialogue.

The conference becomes a turning point in Oliver's career and spiritual life. He begins to work on 'The Bridge of Beliefs' project, integrating architectural designs with elements from various religious symbols and teachings. This project not only enhances his professional legacy but also deepens his personal understanding of the divine, reinforcing his belief that while the paths may differ, the pursuit of higher truth and salvation is a universal journey.

Through Oliver's story, the value of exploring whether all roads lead to heaven is depicted not just in theological debate but in practical, impactful actions that foster greater unity and understanding among diverse populations. His life and projects underscore the belief that in diversity there's beauty and strength, and perhaps, multiple paths leading to the divine.

What is the Difference Between Religion and Relationship?

As we journey further into the labyrinth of faith, we encounter a pivotal crossroads: the distinction between religion and relationship. This is not just a matter of semantics but a profound exploration of how we connect with the divine. It's a question that challenges us to look beyond rituals and doctrines, delving into the heart of what it means to truly experience faith.

Religion: The Path of Traditions and Rituals

Religion, in its myriad forms, is often seen as the roadmap of spirituality. It encompasses the traditions, rituals, and doctrines that have been passed down through generations. Religion offers structure, a sense of community, and a framework for understanding the divine. It's like a well-trodden path through a vast forest, offering guidance and direction.

However, religion can sometimes become more about the path itself than the destination. It can become a series of motions to go through, rites to perform, and rules to follow. When this happens, the essence of faith can be lost in the mechanics of religious practice.

Relationship: The Journey of Personal Connection

On the other side of this spectrum is the concept of relationship—a personal, intimate connection with the divine. This is less about following a predetermined path and more about forging your own. It's about experiencing the divine in a way that is deeply personal and transformative.

A relationship with the divine is characterized by open communication, heartfelt devotion, and a sense of closeness that transcends rituals. It's akin to a friendship or partnership, where the connection is nurtured through personal experiences, honest conversations, and a deep sense of understanding and trust.

The Interplay of Religion and Relationship

The beauty of this journey lies in the understanding that religion and relationships are not mutually exclusive. Religion can be the vessel that carries us towards a deeper, more personal relationship with the divine. It can provide the language, the concepts, and the community that nurture our personal spiritual journey.

At the same time, a personal relationship with the divine can enrich our religious practices, infusing them with deeper meaning and purpose. It can transform rituals from mere routines into expressions of a living, breathing faith.

As we navigate the nuances between religion and relationship, we are invited to reflect on our own spiritual journey. Are we walking a path laid down by tradition, or are we forging a personal connection with the divine? Or perhaps, we are finding a harmonious blend of both. This exploration is a crucial part of understanding the crossroads of belief, where the external world of religion meets the internal world of spiritual relationship.

Abigail's Path from Religion to Relationship

Abigail, a 34-year-old librarian with a gentle demeanor and an insatiable curiosity for spiritual texts, embodies the seeker at the heart of every faith journey. Known in her community for her thoughtful discussions and the delicate silver cross she always wears, Abigail's journey through religion and personal faith encapsulates the quest for a deeper connection with the divine.

Ever since she was a child attending church services with her family, Abigail felt a mixture of awe and distance. She cherished the community and the rituals, yet at night, she'd often feel a gap, a longing for something more personal, more tangible in her spiritual life.

One evening, while organizing a donation box at the library, Abigail finds an old, dusty lantern with intricate patterns etched onto its surface. This lantern, left with a note saying, "Light this to find your way," becomes a symbol for Abigail—a catalyst for her exploration of faith beyond the structured confines of religion.

Abigail begins using the lantern during her nightly reading sessions. One night, with the lantern flickering softly beside her, she delves into a book on personal spiritual experiences. As she reads, she relates deeply with stories of individuals who found profound connections with the divine, not through rituals but through personal moments of revelation and heartfelt prayer.

Inspired by these stories, Abigail decides to use the lantern in a new ritual of her own—nightly meditations focused not on prescribed prayers but on open, honest conversations with the divine. Night after night, with the lantern glowing beside her, Abigail feels a growing sense of closeness and familiarity with the spiritual presence she addresses.

Months later, during a community meeting in her church, Abigail shares her experience. She talks about the old lantern and how it illuminated her path not just through darkness but towards a personal relationship with the divine. She describes her spiritual practices, now deeply enriched with personal significance, yet still harmoniously integrated with her religious community.

Abigail's story becomes a testament in her community, inspiring others to explore personal dimensions of their faith within the framework of their religion. Her journey with the lantern not only bridges her personal faith and communal religion but also lights a way for others to explore the same.

Through Abigail's narrative, the value of understanding the difference between religion and relationship with the divine is vividly illustrated. It shows that while religion provides the structure, personal relationships with the divine fill that structure with life, turning every ritual into a meaningful dialogue and every tradition into a personal testament of faith.

Conclusion

As we draw this chapter to a close, we find ourselves at a pivotal point in our journey of faith. "The Crossroads of Belief" has led us through a labyrinth of challenging ideas and deep spiritual inquiries. We have confronted the most daunting prophecy passages, grappled with the inclusive and exclusive paths to salvation, and explored the delicate balance between religion and personal relationship with the divine.

This exploration has been more than an intellectual exercise; it has been a journey of the heart and soul. We have delved into the depths of our beliefs, questioned long-held assumptions, and faced the complexities of our spiritual convictions. In doing so, we have not only gained a deeper understanding of these profound truths but also of ourselves and our place in the vast tapestry of faith.

As we stand at the crossroads, we are reminded that the journey of faith is never static. It is a dynamic, ever-evolving path that challenges us to grow, question, and seek deeper understanding. The truths we have explored in this chapter are not endpoints but signposts, guiding us towards a more profound, more authentic engagement with our beliefs.

One of the most significant lessons of this chapter is the importance of embracing mystery. The realms of prophecy, salvation, and the divine relationship are shrouded in mystery, and it's in the acceptance of not knowing all the answers that our faith often finds its deepest expression. This mystery invites us to trust, to hope, and to find peace in the assurance that there is more to our spiritual journey than what can be seen or fully understood.

As we conclude this chapter, let us carry forward the insights and questions that have arisen. Let this exploration not end here but continue in our daily lives, in our interactions with others, and in our personal moments of reflection and prayer. Let us use what we have learned as a catalyst for deeper faith, greater compassion, and a more profound understanding of the divine.

We leave "The Crossroads of Belief" not with all the answers, but with a renewed sense of curiosity, a deeper humility, and an invigorated faith. We move forward, knowing that each step on this journey is a step towards greater understanding, deeper connection, and a more authentic expression of our beliefs.

Thank you for walking this path with me. May your journey through the crossroads of belief be enlightening, challenging, and ultimately transformative.

The Sinner's Dilemma: Facing the Truths of Backsliding and Redemption

"If we confess our sins, He is faithful and just and will forgive us our sins and purify us from all unrighteousness." —1 JOHN 1:9 NIV

As we turn the page to chapter three "The Sinner's Dilemma," we embark on a profound exploration of the complexities and nuances of spiritual backsliding and the redemptive journey that follows. This chapter invites us into a candid and empathetic examination of what it means to lose one's way and the transformative process of finding it again.

In the intricate tapestry of faith, the threads of backsliding and redemption are woven with delicate and often unexpected patterns. This chapter is not just about understanding these patterns; it's about recognizing ourselves within them. It's an invitation to confront the truth that we often shy away from—the realities of spiritual faltering and the hopeful promise of redemption.

"The Sinner's Dilemma" takes us through the terrain of human fallibility—the moments of weakness, doubt, and missteps that are inherent in the human experience. We delve into the heart of what causes us to stray from our spiritual paths and the misconceptions that can prolong our journey back. This exploration is a call to understanding, not judgement, recognizing that backsliding is a chapter in almost every believer's story.

Yet, in the midst of these challenges, this chapter also shines a light on the beacon of redemption. We explore the transformative power of grace, forgiveness, and renewed commitment. This is a journey about hope—and the kind of hope that emerges even in our darkest moments, reminding us that redemption is always within reach.

Whether you are someone who has experienced the twists and turns of spiritual backsliding, or a seeker trying to understand the depths of faith, this chapter offers insights that resonate with every step of the spiritual journey. It's a chapter for the lost and the found, for the seekers and the returners, for anyone who has ever wondered about the intricacies of falling and rising in faith.

As we delve into "The Sinner's Dilemma," let us do so with open hearts and minds, ready to embrace the lessons hidden in our faltering's and the joy found in our return. This chapter is an affirmation that in the journey of faith, every setback is a setup for a comeback, and every fall is an opportunity for grace to lift us higher.

3 Mistakes Every Backslider Makes

In the tapestry of faith, the threads of backsliding and redemption are intricately woven, reflecting the complex journey of human spirituality. This chapter delves into the nuanced landscape, exploring the pitfalls and challenges that often accompany the experience of backsliding. Recognizing these mistakes is not about casting judgment; it's about understanding the journey back to redemption, a path marked by grace, learning, and resilience.

Mistake 1: Believing That Slipping Once Means Falling Forever

The journey of faith is rarely a straight line; it is a path filled with ebbs and flows, triumphs and setbacks. The first mistake that many backsliders make is perceiving a single misstep as an irreversible plunge. This belief can be crippling, shrouded in a sense of finality that obscures the truth of spiritual resilience. In truth, faith is characterized by its ability to endure and overcome these stumbles. Each slip is not a final fall; rather, it is a part of human condition, an opportunity for reflection, learning, and growth. Recognizing this can transform our setbacks into stepping stones, guiding us back to the path of faith.

Mistake 2: Underestimating the Power of Grace

Within the heart of many spiritual traditions lies the concept of grace, a powerful, redeeming force that offers renewal and forgiveness. The second common mistake backsliders make is understanding this transformative power. Wrapped in the clutches of guilt and shame, it's easy to view one's actions as beyond redemption. However, this view diminishes the very essence of grace. Grace is not a finite resource, doled out sparingly; it is abundant, ever present, and always accessible. It's a reminder that our spiritual journey is not defined by our failings but our ability to rise above them, to embrace the boundless compassion and forgiveness that grace offers.

Mistake 3: Isolating from the Faith Community

The role of community in the journey of faith cannot be overstated. It is within the embrace of a faith community that we find support, understanding, and guidance. Yet, in times of backsliding, many make the mistake of withdrawing into themselves, shrouded in shame or fear of judgement. This isolation can be a significant barrier to healing and redemption. By distancing themselves from their community, backsliders deprive themselves of a vital source of strength and encouragement. Reconnecting with one's faith community can be a powerful step towards recovery. It is in the shared experiences, the collective wisdom, and the compassionate support of a community that we often find the strength to reclaim our faith and embark on the road to redemption.

This chapter is an invitation to understand and navigate the complexities of backsliding and redemption. It's an exploration aimed at offering hope, insights, and a way back to spiritual wholeness for those who find themselves on this challenging path. As we traverse this terrain, let us do so with empathy, understanding that the journey of faith is a mosaic of experiences, where moments of faltering are as integral as those of triumph.

Lucas's Journey from Backsliding to Belief

Lucas, a 45-year-old school teacher known for his engaging history classes and a knack for coaching soccer, had always been a pillar in his community church. However, a series of personal setbacks, including a divorce and the loss of his mother, saw Lucas retreating from activities he once loved, including his active participation in the church.

The grief and changes overwhelmed Lucas. He felt disconnected not just from his community but from his faith. Each Sunday morning he awoke with the intention to attend service, only to find excuses; his Bible collecting dust on the bedside table. His faith, once a source of strength, now seemed like a distant memory, exacerbating his feelings of failure and detachment.

The turning point came unexpectedly during a weekend soccer match he was coaching. One of his players, a young boy struggling with his parents' recent divorce, broke down after missing what could have been a winning goal. Lucas's heart ached as he consoled the boy, realizing how much he missed being a source of guidance and strength. This moment of empathy jolted Lucas from his spiritual lethargy.

Motivated by the need to overcome his own struggles and to support others, Lucas decided to attend a midweek service. Stepping back into the church, he felt an overwhelming sense of returning home, the familiar hymns and the warmth of shared smiles reigniting something within him.

He confessed his struggles to the pastor afterward, expecting judgment but receiving compassion and understanding instead. The pastor shared his own stories of doubt and recovery, reinforcing the message that backsliding wasn't a perpetual fall but a detour on Lucas's faith journey.

Reenergized by the acceptance and support of his faith community, Lucas started attending a weekly support group within the church. Here, he found others who had faced similar challenges. Their stories of recovery, rooted in grace and communal strength, inspired him to forgive himself and to reengage with his faith more profoundly than before.

Months later, at a community gathering, Lucas shared his journey of backsliding and recovery. His story, filled with moments of despair turned into steps towards healing, resonated with many. His narrative underscored the importance of community and the transformative power of grace, offering hope to those silently struggling.

Lucas's journey from isolation back to active faith participation became a beacon for others in his community. His experience highlighted the fallacy of perpetual failure and the reality of redemption through community support and divine grace. Lucas's renewed faith and active engagement in his church and soccer coaching reaffirmed that backsliding was not an end but a bend in the road, leading to deeper spiritual connections and resilience.

Through Lucas's narrative, the value of understanding the pitfalls of backsliding and embracing the path to redemption is vividly illustrated, showing that while we all may stumble, our falls do not define us—our actions to rise again do.

If You Do These Things, You Will Never Stumble

In the intricate dance of faith and fallibility, there lies a profound truth: while stumbling is part of the human experience, there are practices and principles that can significantly fortify our spiritual walk. This section of our journey is about discovering those actions and attitudes that can create a bulwark against backsliding. It's about laying a foundation so strong that, even in the face of life's tempests, our faith stands unwavering.

Embrace Humility and Self-Reflection

The first cornerstone in this fortification is humility coupled with self-reflection. Humility allows us to acknowledge our limitations and dependences, opening us to the wisdom and guidance that can steer us away from potential pitfalls. Self-reflection is the mirror through which we can regularly examine our actions, motivations, and choices, ensuring they align with our spiritual values. This practice of introspection and humility is a powerful tool in maintaining our footing on the path of faith.

Cultivate a Consistent Prayer or Meditation Practice

Consistency in prayer or meditation is akin to regularly nurturing the soil of our spiritual garden. It creates a space of stillness, contemplation, and connection with the divine. This consistent practice becomes a source of strength and clarity, helping us navigate life's challenges with a centered and grounded spirit. It's in these moments of quietude that we often find the resilience to withstand the storms of temptation and doubt.

Engage in Regular Study and Learning

Faith, like any significant aspect of life, thrives on continuous learning and exploration. Engaging in regular study of spiritual texts, teachings, or even contemporary writings on faith helps us to deepen our understanding and solidify our beliefs. This pursuit of knowledge acts as a safeguard against the confusion and misinterpretation that can lead to backsliding. It empowers us to make informed decisions and approach our spiritual journey with wisdom and discernment.

Foster Meaningful Community Connections

We are not meant to walk the path of faith alone. Fostering meaningful connections within a community of like-minded individuals provides a support system that can uphold us in times of weakness. These relationships offer accountability, encouragement, and a shared experience that can reinforce our commitment to our spiritual journey. A strong, supportive community acts as a buffer against the isolation that can lead to backsliding.

Practice Compassion and Service

Finally, actively practicing compassion and engaging in acts of service aligns our actions with the core tenets of many faiths. By focusing outward on the needs of others, we often find our own spiritual paths strengthened. Service and compassion anchor us in the principles of love, empathy, and altruism, which are potent antidotes to the self-centeredness that can lead to spiritual faltering.

Incorporating these practices into our daily lives builds a foundation of spiritual resilience. While no journey is devoid of challenges, these principles can significantly reduce the likelihood of backsliding, guiding us towards a path of continuous growth and steadfast faith.

Chloe's Journey to Spiritual Renewal

Chloe, a 38-year-old community organizer in a bustling city, has always woven her spirituality tightly with her dedication to social justice. Known for her compassionate nature and unwavering commitment, Chloe's life seemed to mirror her deep faith. However, the pressures of her job and personal life challenges began to erode her spiritual resilience.

Caught between the demands of her profession and her personal aspirations, Chloe felt herself drifting from her spiritual practices. The early morning meditations became sporadic, and her engagement with her faith community waned. She felt an overwhelming sense of being adrift, spiritually disconnected amidst the chaos of her daily routines.

The turning point came during a community rally Chloe organized. The event was aimed at addressing homelessness, a cause close to her heart, but complications arose, threatening to derail the initiative. Overwhelmed and on the verge of giving up, Chloe found herself in the small garden behind the community center, seeking a moment of peace.

As she sat there, the weight of her disconnection bore down on her. It was then that she realized how much her spiritual neglect had affected her ability to handle life's challenges. In that quiet garden, Chloe decided it was time to rebuild her spiritual foundations.

Chloe began dedicating time each morning, not just for rushed meditations, but for deep, reflective self-assessment. She recognized her limitations and sought to understand her role within the larger tapestry of her community and her faith.

This humility opened her up to seeking and accepting support when needed, reinforcing her resilience.

She revitalized her meditation practice, making it a non-negotiable part of her morning ritual. She also rejoined her faith-based study group, which met weekly. This re-engagement provided both spiritual nourishment and a reminder of the shared journey of faith. The community's support was instrumental in reaffirming her commitment to her path.

Chloe integrated her work with her spiritual life by initiating a partnership between her community center and local faith groups. This collaboration not only expanded the reach of her social projects but also aligned her daily work with her spiritual values of compassion and service.

Months later, Chloe stood at another rally, this time with a deep sense of calm and purpose. Her renewed spiritual practices had transformed not just her ability to cope with challenges but had enriched her interactions and effectiveness within her community. Her story of reconnection and resilience inspired others in her community to explore their own spiritual paths, reinforcing the value of a grounded faith journey.

Chloe's journey illustrates that while stumbling may be part of life, the integration of consistent spiritual practices, community support, and a service-oriented life can create a profound bulwark against spiritual backsliding. Her experience serves as a beacon to others, showcasing the transformative power of returning to one's spiritual roots and the profound impact it can have on both personal and community levels.

———————

Where Is the Sinner's Prayer Found in the Bible?

In the mosaic of faith and redemption, one element often sparks curiosity and debate: the Sinner's Prayer. This prayer, seen by many as a pivotal step in the journey of salvation and repentance, is surrounded by questions of its origins and presence in the Bible. Does this prayer, often recited by those seeking redemption, have a direct scriptural basis, or is its genesis found elsewhere?

The Essence of the Sinner's Prayer

The Sinner's Prayer is essentially a personal, heartfelt expression of repentance and acceptance of divine grace. It is a moment of turning, a pivot from one path to another, signifying a deep recognition of one's own shortcomings and a sincere request for forgiveness and guidance. The prayer is a blend of confession, repentance, and commitment to a new path aligned with spiritual teachings.

Searching for a Biblical Foundation

In seeking the scriptural roots of the Sinner's Prayer, one might not find a verbatim passage that lays it out. Instead, the Bible offers various moments and teachings that echo the sentiments and elements of this prayer. We see instances of heartfelt repentance, cries for forgiveness, and declarations of faith, each encapsulating the essence of what the Sinner's Prayer represents.

Biblical Echoes and Examples

Consider the profound humility of the tax collector in Luke 18:13, who, standing afar off, would not so much as lift his eyes to heaven, but beat his breast, saying, "God, be merciful to me a sinner!" This simple, powerful plea captures the essence of repentance and reliance on divine mercy.

In the book of Psalms, we find numerous cries for forgiveness and restoration, like Psalm 51, where David expresses a deep sense of remorse and a longing for renewal. These passages, while not labeled as the Sinner's Prayer, resonate with its spirit and intent.

The Prayer's Role and Impact

While the Sinner's Prayer may not have a single, definitive origin in scripture, its significance in the lives of believers cannot be understated. It marks a profound personal moment of transformation, a conscious decision to embrace a spiritual journey. The prayer, in its many forms, continues to be a powerful expression of faith, repentance, and commitment.

As we explore the roots and expressions of the Sinner's Prayer, we are reminded of the broader truth that faith often transcends the literal words of scripture. It is found in the spirit of the teachings, the heartfelt expressions of repentance, and the personal journeys of transformation that resonate throughout the biblical narrative.

———

Jack's Journey from Skepticism to Renewal

Jack, a 45-year-old auto mechanic from a small town, had long drifted away from the spiritual teachings of his youth. His life, filled with the daily grind and occasional bouts of weekend leisure, seemed typical yet unfulfilled. Known for his pragmatic approach to life and a skeptic's eye for matters of faith, Jack seldom considered the deeper existential questions that once troubled him as a young man.

Jack's journey took a sharp turn following a series of personal crises, including the loss of his job and a difficult breakup. These events plunged him into a state of introspection and existential questioning, bringing him face-to-face with the void his skepticism had masked. The once-dismissed notions of faith and redemption began to echo in his mind, leading him to seek answers and solace once again in the faith he had left behind.

The pivotal moment came unexpectedly one evening at a local community event, where Jack, seeking distraction from his troubles, stumbled upon a small group gathered in a quiet corner, discussing the power of redemption and the concept of the Sinner's Prayer. The group shared stories of personal transformation and discussed the underlying principles found in scripture that mirrored the sentiments of the Sinner's Prayer.

Moved by the stories and warmed by the group's genuine empathy, Jack felt a surge of emotion he hadn't experienced in years. He joined the circle, and for the first time in decades, he opened up about his struggles, his doubts, and his desire for a new beginning. Encouraged by the group, he articulated his own version of the Sinner's Prayer, a heartfelt plea for mercy, guidance, and a new path.

This moment marked a profound change in Jack. It wasn't just about the words of the prayer, but the act of opening his heart and embracing the possibility of transformation. Over the following months, Jack's life took on new meaning. He re-engaged with his community, found solace in regular spiritual gatherings, and even began volunteering, helping others overcome their struggles.

As Jack's journey unfolded, he found that the strength of his renewed faith was amplified by the support of his community. He learned that while the Sinner's Prayer had not been a magic formula, it had served as a crucial stepping stone back to a life of faith and purpose. His story became a testament to the transformative power of personal repentance and the profound impact of spiritual community support.

Jack's experience illustrates the essence of the Sinner's Prayer not as a scriptural mandate but as a personal catalyst for change. His journey from skepticism to faith, catalyzed by his encounter and the simple yet profound act of prayer, highlights the universal quest for redemption and the personal nature of spiritual awakening. His story serves as a beacon to others, showing that renewal is possible, and often, just a sincere prayer away.

Conclusion

As we conclude this introspective journey through chapter three, "The Sinner's Dilemma," We find ourselves at a juncture of profound understanding and renewed hope. This exploration of backsliding and redemption has not just been about uncovering the pitfalls of spiritual journeys; it has been an affirmation of the relentless power of grace and the enduring spirit of human resilience.

We have navigated the complex terrain of spiritual backsliding, recognizing it as a universal experience, not unique to a few but a part of the human condition. In understanding the common mistakes every backslider makes; we have uncovered the threads of compassion and empathy that bind us all in our spiritual quests.

Delving into the practices that fortify us against stumbling, we have rediscovered the timeless tools of faith—humility, reflection, community, and service. These are not just practices but beacons that light our path, guiding us through the fog of doubt and the storms of temptation.

Perhaps most importantly, this chapter has reaffirmed the power of redemption. In exploring the origins and expressions of the Sinner's Prayer, we have seen how redemption is not a distant theological concept but a tangible, accessible reality. It's a testament to the transformative power of faith, a reminder that no matter how far we stray, the path back is always open.

As we close this chapter, let us carry forward the lessons learned, not as mere intellectual insights but as living truths to guide our spiritual walk. Let the understanding of our vulnerabilities make us more compassionate, the awareness of grace more hopeful, and the knowledge of redemption more resilient.

Remember, "The Sinner's Dilemma" is not just a chapter in a book; it's a reflection of the chapters in our lives. The journey of faith is ongoing, filled with highs and lows, stumbles and triumphs. Each step, each faulter, and each recovery is a part of the beautiful tapestry of our spiritual journey.

As we turn the page from this chapter, let us do so with a renewed sense of purpose and a deeper appreciation of the journey. May the truths of backsliding and redemption we've explored here not only enlighten our minds but also fortify our spirits for the path ahead.

CHAPTER FOUR

The Call to Readiness: Preparing to Meet Your Maker

"Examine yourselves to see whether you are in the faith; test yourselves.
Do you not realize that Christ Jesus is in you—unless, of course, you fail
the test." —2 CORINTHIANS 13:5 NIV

As we embark upon chapter four, "The Call to Readiness," we find ourselves at a pivotal juncture in our spiritual journey. This chapter beckons us to contemplate one of the most profound aspects of our faith: our preparedness to meet our Maker. It's a journey that takes us beyond the surface of daily rituals and religious observance, delving into the essence of what it means to be truly ready in our spirit and our being.

THE CALL TO READINESS

"The Call to Readiness" is not just a chapter; it's a journey of self-examination and reflection. It invites us to pause in the midst of our busy lives and ask ourselves some of the most fundamental questions about our faith and existence. Are we living in a way that truly reflects our deepest beliefs? Have we nurtured a spiritual readiness within ourselves? It's a chapter that challenges us to look inward, to assess our spiritual health, and to align our lives more closely with our spiritual ideals.

In this chapter, we also delve deeply into one of the most beautiful and profound concepts of faith: grace. What does the Bible say about grace? How does grace impact our readiness to meet our Maker? We explore the scriptural foundations of grace, understanding it as an unmerited favor, a transformative force, and a guide for our daily living. Grace is the golden thread that weaves through our spiritual fabric, offering hope, strength, and renewal.

Throughout this chapter, we explore what it means to be truly prepared for the ultimate encounter with our Creator. This preparation is not about true fear or trepidation; it is about living with intention, purpose, and a deep sense of spiritual fulfillment. It's about cultivating a life that resonates with the truth of our beliefs, a life that stands ready at any moment to step into the divine presence.

As we journey through "The Call to Readiness," we are called to action. This chapter is an invitation to take tangible steps toward spiritual readiness, to embrace the teachings of grace, and to live each day with a sense of purpose and anticipation. It's a reminder that our readiness to meet our Maker is not just a future concern but a present opportunity.

Let us embark on this chapter with open hearts and minds, ready to explore the depths of our faith and to embrace the call to readiness. May this journey enrich our understanding, deepen our connection with the divine, and inspire us to live each day with spiritual intention and grace.

Are You Ready to Meet the Lord?

As we turn the pages to chapter four, "The Call to Readiness," we embark on a deeply introspective and profoundly significant journey. This chapter beckons us to contemplate a question that resonates at the core of our spiritual being: are we ready to meet our Maker? It's a question that transcends mere philosophical inquiry, touching the very essence of our faith and existence.

The Urgency of Readiness

This pivotal question, "Are you ready?" is not one to be taken lightly. It's a call that echoes with urgency and gravity. In the hustle and bustle of our daily lives, where moments blend into days and days into years, this question jolts us into a state of reflection. It's an invitation to pause, to look inward, and to evaluate the state of our spiritual preparedness.

Examining Our Spiritual State

Are we ready to meet the Lord? This inquiry challenges us to examine our spiritual health, our actions, beliefs, and the alignment of our lives with our spiritual values. It's about taking an honest look at how we live, how we love, and how we serve. This examination is not about inciting fear but about inspiring a journey towards spiritual wholeness and readiness.

The Path to Preparedness

Preparing to meet our Maker is a multifaceted journey. It involves nurturing our relationship with the divine, aligning our actions with our faith, and cultivating a life that reflects our deepest beliefs and values. It's about living each day with intention, and a consciousness of our spiritual calling.

Living with Purpose and Hope

As we delve into this topic, we explore what it means to live a life of purpose, intention, and hope. A life that is ready, at any moment, to stand in the presence of the divine. This readiness is not born out of fear but out of love—a deep, abiding love for our Maker and a sincere desire to live in alignment with that love.

In "Are You Ready to Meet the Lord?" We are invited to embark on a profound and transformative journey. It's a call to readiness that challenges us to live each day with spiritual intentionality, preparing our hearts and minds for the ultimate encounter with our Maker.

Layla's Journey to Spiritual Readiness

Layla, a 32-year-old elementary school teacher from the bustling city of Chicago, found herself caught in the daily grind, her life a blur of lesson plans, grading papers, and fleeting weekends. Known for her dedication to her students and her vibrant classroom presence, Layla often put her personal life and spiritual health on the back burner.

Despite her professional success, Layla felt a nagging sense of incompleteness, a yearning for something deeper that remained unfulfilled. This feeling was amplified by the sudden illness of a close friend, which starkly reminded her of life's fragility and the unanswered questions she harbored about her own spiritual state.

The pivotal moment came on a chilly Sunday morning when Layla, seeking some peace of mind, wandered into a local church. The sermon that day was titled "Are You Ready to Meet the Lord?" The message struck a chord deep within her, stirring the dormant questions she had about her readiness and her relationship with the divine.

As the pastor spoke of living with purpose and readiness, Layla found herself reflecting on her own life. She realized that she had been living without a clear sense of spiritual direction or intention. This moment of realization was profound and marked the beginning of Layla's spiritual awakening.

Motivated by the sermon, Layla began to integrate her spiritual life into her daily routine. She started with small, manageable commitments like daily prayer and participating in weekly Bible studies. These practices deepened her understanding of her faith and gradually aligned her daily life with her spiritual beliefs.

As Layla's journey progressed, she found herself increasingly involved in her church community, connecting with others who shared her path and could offer guidance and support. Her commitment to readiness also led her to engage more actively in service projects, both locally and abroad, which reinforced her sense of purpose and connection to her faith.

Layla's story is a testament to the transformative power of facing one's spiritual state head-on and asking the tough questions about readiness. Her journey from a life of routine to one of deep spiritual intentionality illustrates how anyone, at any point, can begin to prepare themselves to meet their Maker—not out of fear, but out of a profound desire to live a life of purpose and fulfillment.

This narrative encapsulates the essence of the chapter, "The Call to Readiness," showing how the question of readiness can act as a catalyst for profound personal and spiritual growth, guiding individuals toward a path of intentional living and spiritual preparedness.

Reflecting on Life's Journey

In this contemplation of readiness, we are called to reflect on our life journey. How have our choices, our actions, and our relationships shaped our spiritual path? This reflection is an opportunity to assess and realign. It invites us to consider not just what we have done, but who we have become in the process. Have we nurtured qualities like kindness, patience, and empathy? Have we sought to grow in wisdom and understanding? These are the markers of a life preparing to meet its Maker.

Embracing the Moment of Now

The question of readiness also brings our attention to the present moment. It reminds us that preparation for meeting our Maker is not a distant, future task, but a daily, ongoing process. Each day is an opportunity to live in a way that honors our deepest values and beliefs. It's about making choices that reflect our commitment to our spiritual path, finding joy in the journey, and embracing each moment as a precious gift.

The Role of Faith and Trust

At the heart of this readiness is a deep-seated faith and trust. Trust in the divine plan, faith in the journey, and a belief that, no matter the trials and tribulations, there is a purpose and a guiding hand. This faith is not passive; it's active and dynamic. It involves engaging with our beliefs, wrestling with our doubts, and continually seeking a deeper understanding of our spiritual path.

The Promise of Hope

Finally, readiness to meet our Maker is intrinsically linked to hope. It's a hope that transcends the challenges and uncertainties of life, anchoring us in the assurance of something greater than ourselves. This hope is not just a future expectation but a present reality, infusing our daily lives with meaning, purpose, and a sense of divine presence.

As we conclude this exploration of readiness, let us do so with a renewed commitment to our spiritual journey. Let this topic be a catalyst for deep introspection, a renewed focus on living with purpose, and a reinvigoration of our faith and hope. The call to readiness is an ongoing invitation, one that asks us to live each day with an awareness of our ultimate encounter with our Maker.

Benjamin's Path to Spiritual Alignment

Benjamin, a seasoned 58-year-old journalist from New York, found himself at a reflective point in his life. Known for his critical analyses and feature articles that had touched many, Benjamin had spent his career uncovering truths and influencing public opinion. Yet, beneath his professional achievements, he wrestled with personal questions about the spiritual significance of his life's work and his preparedness to meet his Maker.

Benjamin's journey to readiness began on a quiet evening at home, surrounded by stacks of his published works. Despite his success, he felt an unsettling void about the spiritual and personal significance of his life's journey. The accolades were fulfilling, but they didn't answer the deeper questions about his spiritual state and readiness.

The pivotal moment came when Benjamin stumbled upon an old photograph of himself taken during a volunteer mission in his early twenties. The image, showing a young, vibrant version of himself serving in a community kitchen, sparked a profound realization. He remembered the sense of purpose and connection he felt back then—a stark contrast to his current spiritual complacency.

This moment of nostalgia propelled Benjamin into a deep introspective journey. He began to assess his life not by his journalistic achievements but by the qualities he had nurtured—kindness, patience, and empathy. He questioned whether his current lifestyle mirrored the values he truly esteemed.

Motivated by his reflection, Benjamin decided to realign his daily actions with his spiritual beliefs. He resumed volunteering, not just as a weekend activity but as a core part of his life. He also started hosting community discussions, using his skills to foster understanding and empathy among diverse groups. This active engagement renewed his sense of purpose and preparedness.

As Benjamin's journey unfolded, he found himself more involved in his faith community, participating in study groups and spiritual retreats. This reconnection with a community of faith provided him with both support and accountability, reinforcing his daily commitment to live a spiritually aligned life.

Benjamin's story is a vivid illustration of how reflective questioning and a moment of realization can transform one's spiritual journey. It shows that readiness to meet our Maker is not a distant goal but a daily practice of aligning one's life with enduring values and faith. Benjamin's narrative encapsulates the essence of the chapter, highlighting the importance of living with purpose, embracing each moment, and moving forward with hope and trust in the spiritual journey.

What Does the Bible Say About Grace?

In the spiritual tapestry of our journey, grace is a thread of extraordinary significance. It's a concept that permeates the Bible, offering insight and understanding into the character of the divine and our relationship with it. As we explore what the Bible says about grace, we are not merely examining a theological concept; we are uncovering the very heart of our spiritual narrative.

Grace as Unmerited Favor

One of the most profound truths about grace in the Bible is its depiction as unmerited favor. This concept is a cornerstone in understanding grace—it is not something we can earn or deserve; it is freely given. Ephesians 2:8–9 eloquently encapsulates this idea: "For by grace have you been saved through faith, and that not of yourselves: it is the gift of God, not the works, lest anyone should boast." This passage invites us to view grace as a divine gift, an expression of love and mercy that transcends our human efforts and achievements.

Grace and Redemption

The narrative of grace in the Bible is intricately tied to redemption. It's through grace that the path to redemption is made possible. In the story of salvation, grace plays a pivotal role—it is the mechanism by which redemption is offered to humanity. Romans 3:24 explains, "being justified freely by His grace through the redemption that is in Christ Jesus." Here, grace is the foundation upon which our hope and redemption are built.

The Transformative Power of Grace

Grace is not just a static concept; it's dynamic and transformative. The Bible speaks of grace as a force that changes lives, reshapes destinies, and renews spirits. In 2 Corinthians 12:9, we find the powerful words, "My grace is sufficient for you, for my strength is made perfect in weakness." This highlights the transformative power of grace—it enters our weaknesses and turns them into strengths, our failures into lessons, and our trials into triumphs.

Living in Grace

Finally, the Bible guides us on how to live in grace. It's not just an abstract idea but a practical guide for daily living. Titus 2:11–12 offers insight: "For the grace of God that brings salvation has appeared to all men, teaching us that, denying ungodliness and worldly lusts, we should live soberly, righteously, and godly in the present age." Grace, therefore, is also a teacher, guiding us in how we should live and interact with the world around us.

Exploring what the Bible says about grace is a journey into understanding the depth of divine love and compassion. Grace is a reminder of our intrinsic worth in the eyes of the divine, a call to transformation, and a guide for how we live our lives. It is a fundamental aspect of our readiness to meet our Maker, a pillar upon which our spiritual journey rests.

———

Mason's Journey of Renewal and Impact

Mason, a 45-year-old community leader in a bustling urban neighborhood, had dedicated his life to service and advocacy. Despite his efforts to foster change and uplift his community, Mason often felt overwhelmed by the magnitude of the challenges he faced—from poverty to systemic injustice. These hurdles sometimes made him question the impact of his work and his worthiness of any divine favor.

Late one evening, after a particularly challenging community meeting, Mason sat in the quiet of his small office, wrestling with feelings of doubt and inadequacy. His lifelong mission to serve seemed like a drop in the ocean. He wondered if his efforts were enough and if the grace he often read about in scripture was truly meant for someone like him.

The pivotal moment came unexpectedly. While walking through the community center the next day, Mason encountered Maria, a young woman he had mentored. Maria had recently started her own nonprofit, inspired by Mason's dedication and support. She shared how his guidance had been transformative for her, describing it as a 'grace' that changed her life. This encounter was a profound realization for Mason—it was not about earning grace through grand achievements but about the small moments of influence and kindness.

Encouraged by Maria's words, Mason began to see his work in a new light. He recognized that grace was at work not just in monumental successes but in the everyday interactions that shaped the lives around him. This shift in perspective helped him understand grace as an ever-present force, guiding and enriching his life and work.

This realization sparked a significant change in Mason. He started integrating more personal interactions into his daily routine, focusing on mentoring and direct engagement rather than just overarching goals. He began each day with a short prayer, acknowledging his weaknesses and seeking the strength that grace provided, as mentioned in 2 Corinthians 12:9. This new approach not only revitalized his mission but also deepened his spiritual life, making him more resilient and hopeful.

Mason's story exemplifies the transformative power of understanding grace as described in the Bible. It highlights that grace is not contingent on our perfection but is a gift that empowers and uplifts us despite our imperfections. Mason's renewed approach to his community work, infused with this understanding of grace, not only enhanced his effectiveness but also enriched his personal spiritual journey.

Mason's narrative is a vivid illustration of grace as a transformative force in everyday life. His experience echoes the biblical teachings of grace as an unmerited, empowering gift that sustains and strengthens us. Through his story, we see how an authentic engagement with the concept of grace can change not only individual lives but also ripple out to touch entire communities.

Conclusion

As we draw the curtains on chapter four, "The Call to Readiness," we stand at a moment of reflection and profound understanding. This chapter has taken us on a journey deeper into the heart of our spiritual preparation, challenging us to consider how ready we truly are to meet our Maker.

Throughout this chapter, we've explored the essence of what it means to be prepared for the ultimate encounter with the divine. From the introspective question of our readiness to the transformative understanding of grace, we have navigated the depths of what it means to live a life in anticipation of meeting our Creator. This journey has been about more than just theoretical knowledge; it has been a call to internalize and live out the truths we hold dear.

Our exploration of grace has revealed its pivotal role in our spiritual readiness. We've seen how grace is not just a concept to be understood but a reality to be experienced and a force to guide our daily lives. It is through grace that we find the strength to transform, the courage to persevere, and the hope to carry on, even in the face of life's uncertainties.

As we conclude this chapter, we are reminded that the call to readiness is an ongoing, active pursuit. It's about making a conscious choice every day to live in a manner that aligns with our deepest convictions and spiritual aspirations. This readiness is not a state of fear or anxiety about the future, but a state of joyful anticipation, a life lived with purpose, intention, and grace.

Let us carry forward the insights and inspirations from this chapter into our daily lives. May the call to readiness resonate in our actions, our decisions, and our interactions with others. Let it be a reminder to live each day with a sense of purpose, knowing that each moment is an opportunity to prepare ourselves for the ultimate encounter with our Maker.

As we turn the page from "The Call to Readiness," may we do so with a renewed commitment to our spiritual journey. May our hearts be filled with the grace and wisdom to live each day fully, mindfully, and in anticipation of the divine encounter that awaits us.

The Foundations of a Christian Life: Building Blocks for the Believer

"Therefore everyone who hears these words of mine and puts them into practice is like a wise man who built his house on the rock. The rain came down, the streams rose, and the winds blew and beat against that house; yet it did not fall, because it had its foundation on the rock."
—Matthew 7:24–25 NIV

As we embark on chapter five, "The Foundations of a Christian Life," we enter a space of building and nurturing the essential elements of a fulfilling spiritual journey. This chapter is a guide, a compass if you will, for laying down the fundamental blocks that support a robust and vibrant Christian life. It's about constructing a framework of faith that not only stands the test of time but also enriches every facet of our existence.

In this chapter, we explore the core elements that form the bedrock of Christian living. These are not just spiritual concepts but practical tools and virtues that guide believers in their daily walk with Christ. From establishing a home rooted in Christian values to equipping new believers with essential resources for their journey, we delve into what it truly means to live a life anchored in faith.

"Living the Christian Life" is more than just a phrase; it's an invitation to embody the teachings of Christ in our actions, thoughts, and interactions. This chapter seeks to illuminate the path for living out our faith authentically and wholeheartedly. It's about translating belief into action, making our faith visible in the way we live our lives.

The importance of a Christian home cannot be overstated. "The 10 Commandments of a Christian Home" provides a blueprint for creating an environment where faith is nurtured, love is abundant, and Christian values are lived out daily. It's about making our homes centers of spiritual growth, love, and grace.

For those new to faith, "Every New Christian Needs 7 Things" offers a treasure trove of wisdom and guidance. This section is designated to equip new believers with the tools, understanding, and support they need to embark on their spiritual journey confidently and purposefully.

Chapter five is a journey through the fundamental aspects of Christian living. It's a chapter for those looking to deepen their faith, for families striving to create a God-centered home, and for new believers seeking direction on their spiritual path. Let's embark on this journey together, building and strengthening our faith, step by step, block by block.

Living the Christian Life

As we step into chapter five, "The Foundations of a Christian Life," we embark on a journey to explore the essential building blocks of living a life in Christ. This chapter is not just a roadmap; it's a deep dive into the heart and soul of what it means to live out our faith in every aspect of our existence.

The Essence of Christian Living

Living the Christian life is about so much more than adherence to rituals and recitation of prayers. It's a transformative experience that permeates every facet of our being. This journey takes us beyond the walls of the church and into the world, where our faith is not just professed but actively practiced. It's about embodying the principles of love, grace, and compassion that are central to the Christian faith.

Faith in Action

In this exploration, we delve into the concept of faith in action. Christian living is a dynamic interplay of belief and behavior, where our convictions are reflected in our actions. It's about making choices that align with our values, engaging in acts of service and kindness, and living in a way that illuminates the path for others. This is where faith moves from being a personal belief to a visible, tangible force in the world.

Nurturing a Personal Relationship with God

At the core of living the Christian life is the nurturing of a personal relationship with God. This relationship is the bedrock upon which all other aspects of Christian living are built. It's fostered through prayer, meditation, study of the scriptures, and a continual seeking of God's presence in our lives. This intimate connection with the divine guides us, sustains us, and provides a source of unending strength and wisdom.

The Challenge of Consistency

One of the greatest challenges in living the Christian life is maintaining consistency. It's easy to be a Christian in moments of tranquility and comfort, but the true test lies in being steadfast in times of trials and tribulations. This chapter explores how to cultivate a faith that is constant, a belief that does not waver when faced with the complexities and challenges of everyday life.

A Community of Believers

Finally, living the Christian life is not a solitary journey. It is enriched and strengthened by the community of believers. Fellowship with other Christians provides support, accountability, and a shared experience of faith. It's in the communion with others that our individual faith is nurtured and our collective strength is bolstered.

In "Living the Christian Life," we uncover the fundamental aspects of what it means to walk in faith, to live a life that not only believes in Christ but also emulates His teachings. This is the journey of building a life upon the solid foundation of Christian principles, a life that stands as a testament to the power and beauty of our faith.

Nora's Journey from Sunday Observance to Daily Practice

Nora, a 33-year-old elementary school teacher in a vibrant urban community, had always been a "Sunday Christian," her faith confined within the walls of her church each weekend. Despite her regular attendance, her weekdays were untouched by her spiritual life, leading to a growing sense of disconnect and superficiality in her faith.

Nora's turning point came one autumn evening while grading papers. She realized that while she taught her students about integrity and kindness, she rarely practiced these values beyond surface-level interactions. This realization brought a profound sense of emptiness and a yearning for a deeper, more authentic Christian life.

The pivotal moment unfolded unexpectedly in her classroom. During a heated exchange between two students, instead of the usual protocol, Nora found herself calming the children by sharing a personal story about forgiveness and reconciliation—principles she had learned but seldom practiced. This incident was her epiphany; it wasn't enough to teach values, she needed to embody them.

Motivated by this experience, Nora began to integrate her faith into her daily life actively. She started a morning routine of prayer and Bible reading, which she had often neglected. In her classroom, she implemented a "kindness corner," where students could write down acts of kindness they observed or experienced, celebrating them weekly.

This new approach transformed Nora's life and teaching. Her relationships with her students deepened, and her classroom became a model for the school, known for its atmosphere of respect and compassion. Nora's faith became her guide, not just in personal matters but in her professional life, making her a beacon of hope and a role model in her community.

Nora's story illustrates the profound impact of integrating faith into everyday life. It highlights that living the Christian life means more than just attending church; it's about making faith a living, breathing part of every day. Through her journey, Nora discovered that her actions could teach far more about Christianity than words ever could, embodying the principles of love, grace, and compassion in her daily interactions.

Nora's narrative is a compelling example of how the foundations of Christian living can transform not only individuals but also the communities around them. Her journey from a Sunday Christian to a full-time believer in action reflects the transformative power of truly living out one's faith. Through her story, we see how the core principles of Christianity can be woven into the fabric of everyday life, creating a ripple effect that extends far beyond the individual.

———————

The 10 Commandments of a Christian Home

As we delve deeper into the essence of a Christian life, we arrive at a cornerstone of faith lived out within the walls of our homes. "The 10 Commandments of a Christian Home" is not just a list of rules, but a blueprint for nurturing a household grounded in faith, love, and Christian values. These commandments offer guidance for creating a home that is not only a sanctuary of peace and love but also a beacon of Christian witness.

1. Love as the Foundation

The first commandment is to establish love as the foundation of the home. Love, as depicted in 1 Corinthians 13, is patient, kind, and selfless. A Christian home thrives on this love, creating an environment where each member feels valued, understood, and supported.

2. Faith at the Forefront

Keeping faith at the forefront is the second commandment. This means prioritizing spiritual growth through prayer, scripture reading, and Christian teachings. It's about making faith a daily part of life, a constant in the routines of the household.

3. Forgiveness as a Practice

Forgiveness is the third commandment. In a Christian home, mistakes are seen as opportunities for grace and growth. Forgiveness mirrors the mercy we receive from God and is essential for maintaining harmony and understanding within the family.

4. Honoring One Another

The fourth commandment emphasizes honoring one another. This includes respecting individual differences, valuing each other's opinions, and celebrating each other's achievements. It's about acknowledging the divine image in every family member.

5. Cultivating Gratitude

Gratitude is the fifth commandment. A Christian home recognizes the blessings in everyday life, fostering an attitude of thankfulness and contentment. This means regularly expressing appreciation for each other and for God's provision.

6. Service to Others

Service to others, the sixth commandment, extends the love of the family to the community. It's about being a helping hand

and a source of comfort to those in need, reflecting Christ's love through acts of kindness and charity.

7. Fostering Unity

The seventh commandment is fostering unity. In a Christian home, unity is cultivated through shared activities, open communication, and a commitment to resolve conflicts with love and understanding.

8. Nurturing Hope and Joy

The eighth commandment involves nurturing hope and joy. It's about maintaining a positive outlook, celebrating life's joys, and providing comfort during challenging times, always anchored in the hope that comes from faith.

9. Instilling Discipline and Responsibility

The ninth commandment is about instilling discipline and responsibility. This includes setting boundaries, teaching the value of hard work, and guiding family members to be responsible and contentious individuals.

10. Living as Witnesses

Finally, the tenth commandment is living as witnesses. A Christian home serves as a testament to faith, demonstrating through everyday actions the transformative power of living a Christ-centered life.

These 10 commandments offer a framework for building a home that not only nurtures its members spiritually but also shines as an example of Christian living. They are not just guidelines but stepping stones to creating a household that glorifies God in all aspects.

The Johnsons' Journey
to a Spiritually Enriched Household

Meet the Johnsons: Carter, a 42-year-old community center director, his wife Ella, a 38-year-old school teacher, and their two children, Henry and Ruby, ages 10 and 8. The Johnsons, residing in a bustling suburban neighborhood, had always sought to integrate their Christian faith into their daily lives but found the challenge of truly embodying this in their home life daunting.

The Johnsons felt something was missing in their family dynamic. Despite their efforts, their home often felt more like a logistics hub—full of activity but lacking in deeper, spiritual connections. This realization brought a yearning for a home where faith wasn't just another checkbox but the foundation of their family life.

The pivotal moment came one rainy Saturday morning during a family meeting in their cozy living room. Carter and Ella introduced the idea of the "10 Commandments of a Christian Home," a concept they encountered in a recent church workshop. They decided as a family to commit to these principles, hoping to cultivate a more spiritually enriched home.

1. **Love as the Foundation:** The Johnsons started with family affirmations, taking turns at dinner to express appreciation for one another.

2. **Faith at the Forefront:** They designated Wednesday nights for Bible study, turning them into engaging family discussions on scripture.

3. **Forgiveness as a Practice:** Ella initiated a "forgiveness jar," where family members could leave notes to resolve misunderstandings, teaching forgiveness in action.

4. **Honoring One Another:** Carter implemented one-on-one time with each child every week, ensuring they felt valued individually.

5. **Cultivating Gratitude:** The family began a gratitude board in their kitchen, where they pinned notes of thankfulness daily.

6. **Service to Others:** They volunteered monthly at a local food bank, extending their family's warmth to the community.

7. **Fostering Unity:** Family game nights every Friday helped strengthen their bond, emphasizing teamwork and unity.

8. **Nurturing Hope and Joy:** They started a tradition of sharing personal and spiritual victories during Sunday lunches to nurture joy and hope.

9. **Instilling Discipline and Responsibility:** Chores were assigned not just as tasks but as lessons in responsibility, linked with biblical principles of stewardship.

10. **Living as Witnesses:** The Johnsons invited neighbors to several home-hosted community prayer gatherings, becoming known for their hospitality and faith.

This new approach transformed the Johnson household into a vibrant hub of Christian practice and joy. Their home became a sanctuary where each member felt deeply connected, not only to each other but to their faith. It became a model in their community, inspiring other families with the visible change in how they lived and loved.

The Johnsons' story is a vivid illustration of how the "10 Commandments of a Christian Home" can revolutionize not just the physical space of a home but the spiritual heartbeat of a family. Their journey from a logistical hub to a spiritual hub exemplifies how deeply faith can influence daily living, turning ordinary interactions into profound spiritual connections. Through their story, we see how a home can be transformed into a testament of living faith, impacting everyone who crosses its threshold.

Every New Christian Needs 7 Things

As we journey further into the foundations of a Christian life, we come upon an essential guide for those beginning their walk in faith. "Every New Christian Needs 7 Things" is more than a list; it's a compass for navigating the initial steps of a life changing spiritual journey. These seven essentials are not just resources; they are beacons that light the path for new believers, guiding them towards a fulfilling and robust Christian life.

1. A Bible for Guidance

The first essential is a Bible. It's not just a book, but a living guide, rich with wisdom, truth, and encouragement. For the new Christian, the Bible is the primary source of understanding God's word, an invaluable tool for growth and learning in faith.

2. A Prayerful Heart

Second is the need for a prayerful heart. Prayer is the lifeline between the believer and God, a channel for communication and connection. New Christians are encouraged to cultivate a habit of regular prayer, using it as a means to express gratitude, seek guidance, and find comfort..

3. A Faith Community

Third on the list is a faith community. Christianity is not a solitary journey; it thrives in community. Being part of a church or a group of believers provides essential support, fellowship, and a sense of belonging. It's within this community that faith is nurtured and strengthened.

4. A Heart for Service

Service to others is the fourth essential; it's through acts of love and service that faith becomes active and tangible. Few Christians are encouraged to seek opportunities to serve, reflecting Christ's love and compassion in their actions.

5. Discipleship and Mentorship

Fifth is the need for discipleship and mentorship. Growing in faith often requires guidance and wisdom from those more experienced in the Christian walk. Mentors and discipleship programs can provide invaluable support, teaching, and encouragement to new believers.

6. A Commitment to Growth

The sixth essential is a commitment to growth. Just like any other aspect of life, spiritual maturity requires intention and effort. New Christians should be encouraged to continually seek knowledge, understanding, and deepening of their faith.

7. An Understanding of Grace

Finally, understanding and embracing grace is crucial. Grace is at the heart of the Christian message; it's the recognition that salvation is a gift, not earned but given. New Christians benefit greatly from grasping this fundamental truth, as it shapes their understanding of God and their spiritual journey.

These seven essentials are foundational for every new Christian, providing the tools and guidance needed to embark on a fruitful and enriching spiritual journey. They are not just steps but a holistic approach to embracing and living out a life of faith.

———————

Alice's Journey as a New Believer

Meet Alice, a 28-year-old graphic designer from the bustling city of Atlanta. Having recently attended a life-altering service at a local community church, Alice, stirred by the message of hope and renewal, decided to embrace Christianity. Her journey of faith, however, was fraught with questions, uncertainties, and a deep desire to find her path in this new world.

Alice's transition into faith was filled with both excitement and anxiety. She felt a profound need for guidance and support as she navigated this new chapter in her life. The prospect of deepening her understanding of Christianity was both thrilling and daunting. She longed for something concrete to help ground her burgeoning faith.

The pivotal moment came when Alice attended her second service at the church. She was given a "New Believer's Welcome Kit," which included a contemporary translation of the Bible, a prayer journal, and a list of community groups she could join. This simple gift was her first tangible step towards building her new life in faith.

1. **A Bible for Guidance:** The Bible in her kit became her daily companion. Through its passages, Alice found words of encouragement and answers to her lingering doubts. It guided her thoughts and actions as she began to view the world through a lens of faith.

2. **A Prayerful Heart:** The prayer journal encouraged Alice to make prayer a routine. Morning and night, she poured out her heart to God, finding peace and a growing connection with Him.

3. **A Faith Community:** Alice joined a small group for new believers. Here, she formed friendships with others who were also exploring their faith. This community became her spiritual family, offering support and understanding as she navigated her new beliefs.

4. **A Heart for Service:** Inspired by her group's monthly community outreach, Alice began volunteering at a local food bank. This service became a practical expression of her faith, fulfilling her desire to make a meaningful impact.

5. **Discipleship and Mentorship:** Alice sought mentorship from the leader of her small group, who provided personal guidance and shared wisdom from their own faith journey. This relationship deepened her understanding and enriched her spiritual growth.

6. **A Commitment to Growth:** Alice attended workshops and seminars offered by her church, eager to learn more and strengthen her faith. Each session built upon her

knowledge and inspired her to explore deeper theological concepts.

7. **An Understanding of Grace:** Through her studies and discussions, Alice learned about the grace of God—unearned, freely given, and transformative. This understanding of grace became the bedrock of her faith, offering comfort and assurance in her moments of self-doubt.

Alice's story is a vivid illustration of how the seven essentials for every new Christian can profoundly impact a newcomer to faith. These essentials helped transform her initial uncertainty into a confident, active pursuit of a spiritual life. Alice's journey shows how practical tools and community support can guide new believers towards a fulfilling and resilient Christian life, making the abstract elements of faith a tangible reality.

Conclusion

As we bring chapter five, "The Foundations of a Christian Life," to a close, we reflect on the journey we've taken through the vital building blocks of a believer's life. This chapter has been a journey of discovery and affirmation, exploring the core elements that underpin a vibrant and meaningful Christian existence.

We've delved into what it means to truly live the Christian life, an experience that goes far beyond Sunday worship and into the very fabric of our daily existence. We've learned that our faith is not just a belief system but a way of life, encompassing how we love, serve, and interact with the world around us.

"The 10 Commandments of a Christian Home" have offered us a blueprint for creating a sanctuary of faith, love, and Christian values. This exploration reminds us that our homes are not just physical structures but spiritual havens where faith can flourish, values are nurtured, and love is cultivated.

For those beginning their walk in faith, "Every New Christian Needs 7 Things" has provided essential guidance. This section has been a beacon for new believers, illuminating the path with crucial resources and wisdom to embark confidently on their spiritual journey.

As we conclude this chapter, we are reminded that the foundations of a Christian life are not static; they are continuously built and strengthened over time. Our journey in faith is an ongoing process of learning, growing, and deepening our connection with God and with each other.

Let us carry the lessons and insights from this chapter into our daily lives. May the principles and practices we've explored here serve as steady guides in our journey, helping us to live out our faith with authenticity and purpose.

As we turn the page from "The Foundations of a Christian Life," may we do so with renewed commitment and enthusiasm for our spiritual growth. May our journey be one of learning, faith, and deep love for God and each other.

The Journey of Salvation: Navigating Intellect, Emotions, and Will

"Do not conform to the pattern of this world, but be transformed by the renewing of your mind. Then you will be able to test and approve what God's will is—His good, pleasing and perfect will." —ROMANS 12:2 NIV

Welcome to chapter six, "The Journey of Salvation," a chapter that invites us on an explorative path through the intricate landscapes of intellect, emotions, and will in the context of our spiritual journey. Here, we delve into the profound interplay between these facets of our being and how they shape our response to the most pivotal message of the Christian faith—the Gospel.

The journey of salvation is a complex and deeply personal one. It is not merely a moment of decision but an ongoing process of understanding, feeling, and choosing. This chapter seeks to unravel how our intellect questions and seeks understanding, how our emotions react and connect, and how our will decides and commits in response to the Gospel.

We begin by exploring the role of the intellect and salvation. The intellect, with its capacity for reason and critical thinking, often leads the way in our spiritual exploration. It's through our intellect that we grapple with theological concepts, seek answers to profound spiritual questions, and build a foundation of understanding.

Next, we turn to the realm of emotions, the heart's deep and often immediate response to the Gospel. Our emotions can range from joy and peace to fear and guilt, reflecting the deeply personal impact of the Gospel message. Understanding our emotional responses is crucial as they often guide our steps along with the path of faith.

Finally, we consider the will—the aspect of our being that involves decision and action. In the journey of salvation, the will plays a decisive role. It is the will that ultimately says 'yes' or 'no' to the call of the Gospel, that chooses to embrace or reject the path laid before us.

As we navigate through "The Journey of Salvation: Navigating Intellect, Emotions, and Will," we embark on a journey that is as challenging as it is enlightening. This chapter invites us to understand and engage with the multifaceted nature of our response to salvation, encouraging a deeper and more holistic approach to our faith.

Let us step into this exploration with open minds and hearts, ready to discover the rich interplay between our intellect, emotions, and will on the path of salvation. May this journey bring clarity, insight, and a deeper understanding of our personal walk with faith.

Salvation and Your Intellect, Emotions, and Will

As we embark on chapter six, "The Journey of Salvation," we delve into a profound exploration of how salvation intertwines with the complex tapestry of our intellect, emotions, and will. This chapter is not just an exploration; it's a journey into the depths of our being, understanding how these integral aspects of ourselves interact with the transformative experience of salvation.

The Role of Intellect in Salvation

Our journey begins with intellect, the realm of reason and understanding. Salvation is often perceived as a matter of the heart, but the intellect plays a crucial role in the spiritual journey. It's through our intellect that we grapple with the truths of faith, question our long-held beliefs, and seek understanding of the profound mysteries of salvation. This section explores how our mind engages with the concept of salvation, how it processes the profound truths of faith, and how intellectual exploration can lead to a deeper understanding and acceptance of salvation.

Emotions: The Heart's Response to Salvation

Next, we venture into the world of emotions, the heart's response to the experience of salvation. Emotions are a powerful aspect of our salvation journey. They color our experiences, shape our perceptions, and often guide our reactions to the profound changes that salvation brings into our lives. This part of the chapter delves into how our emotional responses to salvation—joy, doubt, peace, and sometimes turmoil—play a crucial role in our spiritual growth and understanding.

The Will: Choosing the Path of Salvation

Lastly, we examined the will, the aspects of ourselves that involves the decision-making and choice. Salvation is a journey that involves a significant act of the will—the choice to accept, to surrender, and to follow. It's about the decisions we make in response to the call of faith, and how our will is exercised and strengthened as we navigate the path of salvation. This section explores the dynamics of choosing salvation, the ongoing commitment it requires, and how our will is integral to maintaining and deepening our faith journey.

In "Salvation and Your Intellect, Emotions, and Will," we are invited to examine the multifaceted nature of our journey to salvation. This exploration is about understanding and harmonizing the roles of our mind, heart, and will in the transformative experience of salvation. It's a journey that acknowledges the complexity of our beings, and the profound impact salvation has on every part of us.

─────────

Owen's Journey of Rational and Spiritual Discovery

Owen, a 34-year-old software developer from Seattle, found himself at a professional high but a personal and spiritual low. With a mind sharpened by logic and reason, he often dismissed spiritual discussions as emotional rhetoric without basis in rational thought. Yet, deep down, Owen felt an emptiness, a longing for something beyond the tangible successes he had achieved.

Late one evening, while working overtime on a critical project, Owen stumbled upon an online forum discussing the scientific and philosophical underpinnings of faith. His curiosity piqued, he found himself drawn into the depth of the conversation, marking the beginning of an intellectual and emotional journey towards understanding salvation.

It was during an intense discussion on the forum that Owen encountered a compelling argument about the logical consistency of faith and the role of grace in Christianity. This discussion was the catalyst for a profound shift in his perspective. For the first time, his intellect engaged with the concept of salvation not as a mere emotional crutch but as a credible belief system worthy of rational consideration.

1. **Intellectual Engagement:** Owen began to devour books and articles that bridged science, philosophy, and religion.

His intellectual journey was rigorous, challenging his skepticism and opening his mind to new possibilities.

2. **Emotional Surge:** As his understanding deepened, Owen felt an unexpected surge of emotion during a quiet moment of reflection. He experienced what many describe as a "peace that surpasses all understanding," which overwhelmed him in a way logic never could.

3. **Decision of Will:** Faced with the undeniable impact of these experiences on his heart and mind, Owen made a conscious decision. He chose to attend a local church, seeking to integrate his newfound intellectual and emotional understanding with real-life community and practice.

4. **Community Integration:** Within the church, Owen found not only a community that welcomed his questions and embraced his journey but also opportunities to serve others. This integration solidified his faith as he put his beliefs into action, enhancing his emotional connection and commitment to his new path.

5. **Continued Growth:** Owen committed to regular discussions with a mentor, further intertwining his intellect, emotions, and will in the pursuit of deepening his faith. Each step reinforced the other, creating a robust framework for his continuing spiritual journey.

Owen's story illustrates the profound impact of engaging intellect, emotions, and will in the journey of salvation. His experience highlights how each component can not only coexist but profoundly enrich one's spiritual life. Owen's journey from skepticism to faith shows that the path to salvation is multifaceted, requiring the engagement of our entire being. His transformation is a testament to the power of integrating mind, heart, and will in the pursuit of spiritual truth and fulfillment.

Integrating Intellect, Emotions, and Will in Faith

As we delve deeper into understanding how our intellect, emotions, and will interact with our salvation experience, we uncover the intricate balance required to integrate these facets of our being in our faith journey. Salvation is not a one-dimensional experience; it's multifaceted, involving every aspect of who we are.

Intellect: The Gateway to Deeper Understanding

Our intellect is often the starting point in our journey of faith. It's through intellectual curiosity and questioning that many of us begin to explore the truths of Christianity. This exploration, however, is not just about acquiring knowledge; it's about seeking wisdom and understanding. The intellect challenges us to look beyond simple answers, to grapple with difficult questions, and to embrace the mysteries of faith with an open mind.

Emotions: The Authentic Response to Faith

Emotions play a crucial role in our salvation experience. They are our authentic response to the understanding and acceptance of faith. Joy, peace, gratitude, and even sorrow or doubt are all part of the emotional tapestry of our salvation journey. These emotions are a natural response to the profound changes and realizations that come with embracing faith. They connect us deeply to our spiritual experiences, making them more vivid and real.

Will: The Commitment to Follow

The will is where our choices and actions come into play. It's one thing to understand and feel; it's another to act. The will is where our faith moves from thought and feeling into concrete action. It involves the daily choices we make to live out our faith, to follow the teachings of Christ, and to grow in our spiritual journey. The exercise of our will and choosing the path of salvation is a testament to the strength and sincerity of our faith.

Harmonizing These Aspects in Our Spiritual Walk

Bringing together intellect, emotions, and will in our spiritual walk is key to a balanced and mature Christian life. Each aspect has its place and purpose. Our intellect guides us to truth, our emotions give depth to our experience, and our will drives us to action. Together, they form a comprehensive approach to understanding and living out our salvation.

As we conclude this topic, let us embrace the full spectrum of our being in our journey of faith. May our intellect challenge us to grow, our emotions connect us deeply to our spiritual experiences, and our will empower us to live out our faith with conviction and purpose.

Sienna's Path to Intellectual and Spiritual Integration

Sienna, a 28-year-old school teacher in Austin, Texas, found herself at a spiritual crossroads. Raised in a family that valued intellectual rigor over religious commitment, Sienna had always approached life with a questioning mind. Despite her analytical nature, recent personal challenges had stirred a depth of emotion that she struggled to reconcile with her intellectual understanding of the world.

After a particularly trying semester, Sienna felt an overwhelming sense of burnout and existential questioning. She longed for peace and coherence between her intellectual doubts, emotional turbulence, and emerging spiritual curiosity.

The turning point came when Sienna attended a workshop on "Integrating Mind, Heart, and Spirit" at a local community center. It was here, during a quiet meditation session, that Sienna experienced a profound moment of clarity. She realized that her intellect, emotions, and budding spiritual awareness could be harmoniously integrated, not perpetually at odds.

Steps to Integration:

1. **Intellectual Curiosity:** Sienna began attending a study group that explored the historical and philosophical underpinnings of Christianity. This satisfied her intellectual curiosity and gave her a structured way to approach her spiritual questions.

2. **Emotional Engagement:** During the workshop, Sienna connected with a counselor who specialized in spiritual and emotional integration. Through regular sessions, she learned to identify and express her emotions related to faith, allowing her to process her feelings more deeply.

3. **Active Will:** Inspired by her new insights, Sienna decided to volunteer at a local charity, aligning her actions with her growing conviction about the importance of service in Christian teachings. This active expression of faith solidified her commitment and provided practical experiences of her beliefs in action.

4. **Community Support:** Sienna found tremendous support in a small church community that valued both intellectual inquiry and emotional expression. This community became her spiritual home, where she could discuss her doubts openly and receive encouragement.

5. **Continual Growth:** Committed to her path, Sienna integrated daily practices such as prayer and scriptural reflection, which nurtured her intellect, soothed her emotions, and strengthened her will to live out her faith.

Sienna's story highlights the transformative power of integrating intellect, emotions, and will in the faith journey. Her experience illustrates how each component is essential and how together, they provide a fuller, more balanced approach to living a Christian life. Sienna's journey from skepticism to integrated faith shows how embracing all facets of one's being can lead to a profound and harmonious spiritual life.

―――――――

Four Ways People Respond to the Gospel

In our ongoing exploration of the journey of salvation, we now turn our attention to the diverse ways in which people respond to the Gospel. This part of the chapter is not just an observation; it's a deep dive into the human psyche, understanding the myriad reactions to the profound message of the Gospel. The way people respond to this message is as varied as humanity itself, each response reflecting a unique interplay of intellect, emotions, and will.

1. Intellectual Curiosity and Skepticism

The first response is often characterized by intellectual curiosity or skepticism. For some, the Gospel presents a puzzle, effective claims that ignite a spark of curiosity. These individuals approached the Gospel with questions, seeking to understand, analyze, and even challenge its assertions. This intellectual engagement is a crucial part of their journey, as it can lead to a deeper understanding and, eventually, a reasoned conviction in their faith.

2. Emotional Resonance and Connection

Another common response is an emotional one. The Gospel can evoke a powerful emotional reaction in people, striking chords of hope, love, and sometimes even guilt or fear. For these individuals, the message of the Gospel resonates on a deeply emotional level, and their journey towards salvation is often guided by these feelings. This emotional connection can be the catalyst for a profound personal transformation.

3. Indifference or Apathy

A third response to the Gospel is indifference or apathy. In a world brimming with information and competing worldviews, some may hear the Gospel but remain unaffected or uninterested. This response can be due to various factors—a contentment with current beliefs, a preoccupation with their daily life, or a lack of understanding of the Gospel's relevance to their personal experience.

4. Active Rejection or Opposition

Finally, there are those who actively reject or oppose the Gospel. This response can stem from a variety of reasons—

conflicting beliefs, negative experiences with religion, or a strong disagreement with the tenets of the Gospel. For these individuals, the Gospel challenges their current worldview, leading to a defensive or confrontational stance.

Each of these responses to the Gospel reveals a complex interplay of intellect, emotions, and will in our spiritual journeys. Understanding these responses help us to empathize with others in their spiritual quests and to navigate our own responses to the Gospel more mindfully.

In "Four Ways People Respond to the Gospel," we seek to understand and respect the diverse ways people engage with one of the most profound messages they will ever encounter. It's a reminder that the journey of salvation is personal and varied, reflecting the rich tapestry of human experience.

Sebastian's Path to Embracing Faith

Sebastian, a 35-year-old software developer in Seattle, is a man known for his analytical mind and a somewhat reserved demeanor. Having grown up in a non-religious family, he always prided himself on his logical approach to life's questions. However, recent life events—such as the birth of his daughter and the passing of a close friend—had stirred a curiosity about life's deeper meanings.

One evening, while attending a community support group to cope with his grief, Sebastian was introduced to the Gospel for the first time. The message, filled with talk of hope and redemption, triggered a mix of curiosity and skepticism in him.

During one of the meetings, a member shared a poignant experience about finding solace in their faith during tough times. This story struck a chord with Sebastian, sparking a profound emotional reaction he hadn't anticipated. It was a moment of vulnerability and a crack in his armor of skepticism that made him pause and consider the possibilities of faith.

Sebastian's Journey:

1. **Intellectual Curiosity:** Sebastian began to explore the Gospel with his typical analytical rigor. He attended a few more sessions, asking pointed questions and seeking logical explanations to theological concepts. His curiosity led him to read extensively, both scriptures and critical analyses, as he sought to understand the intellectual foundations of Christianity.

2. **Emotional Connection:** Despite his initial resistance, Sebastian found himself increasingly moved by the personal stories shared by members of his group. These stories, filled with themes of forgiveness and new beginnings, began to resonate with him, offering comfort and a new perspective on his own losses.

3. **Confronting Indifference:** While part of him found these explorations meaningful, another part remained indifferent, accustomed to keeping emotional distance. This internal conflict was a significant hurdle, as Sebastian struggled to reconcile his emotional responses with his intellectual conclusions.

4. **Reaching a Decision:** After months of wrestling with his thoughts and feelings, Sebastian experienced a moment of clarity during a quiet night at home. It wasn't a dramatic conversion but a gentle acknowledgment of his desire for faith, a conscious decision to embrace the Gospel not just with his mind but with his heart and will.

Sebastian's story illustrates the transformative power of engaging with the Gospel through intellect, emotions, and will. His journey from skepticism to acceptance showcases the varied responses one can have to the Gospel and the profound impact it can have on an individual's life. Through Sebastian's experience, we see how an initial intellectual curiosity can evolve into an emotional connection and a deliberate choice to embrace a new path of faith.

=====

Conclusion

As we conclude chapter six, "The Journey of Salvation," we reflect on the profound and multifaceted nature of our spiritual odyssey. This chapter has been a deep dive into the interplay between our intellects, emotions, and will in the context of our faith journey, revealing the complexity and beauty of the path to salvation.

We have explored the intricate roles played by our intellect, emotions, and will and responding to the Gospel. Each of these aspects of our being contributes to a rich tapestry of experiences and decisions that define our spiritual journey. The intellect challenges and deepens our understanding, the emotions connect us authentically to our faith, and the will empowers us to live out our beliefs.

Through our exploration of the various ways people respond to the Gospel, we've gained insights into the diverse spiritual landscapes that individuals navigate. This understanding fosters empathy and respect for the varied paths that people take in their journey toward faith, reminding us that each journey is unique and sacred.

This chapter has been an invitation to embrace the complexity of our spiritual selves. It encourages us not to shy away from the challenging questions of the intellect, the deep stirrings of the heart, or the decisive power of the will. Instead, we are called to engage with each aspect fully, integrating them into a cohesive and dynamic faith journey.

As we move forward from this chapter, let us do so with a heightened awareness of how our thoughts, feelings, and choices shape our relationship with the divine. May we continue to navigate our journey of salvation with intention, depth, and a holistic understanding of our spiritual nature.

Chapter six has been a journey not just of understanding but of self-discovery. As we turn the page, let us carry with us the insights and reflections we've gathered, using them to enrich our walk of faith, to deepen our connection with the divine, and to illuminate our path as we continue our spiritual journey.

The Pathway Marked Out: Unpacking the Roman Road and Spiritual Laws

"For the wages of sin is death, but the gift of God is eternal life in Christ Jesus our Lord." —ROMANS 6:23 NIV

Welcome to chapter seven, "The Pathway Marked Out," where we embark on a journey of discovery and understanding through two of the most significant frameworks in Christian evangelism—the Roman Road and the Four Spiritual Laws. This chapter is not just a study; it's an explorative journey that weaves through scripture, unveiling the profound truths about salvation and our personal walk with God.

We begin with the Roman Road, a path marked out through the verses of Paul's Epistle to the Romans. This road is a beacon for many, guiding them to a deeper understanding of salvation. It's a journey that takes us through the essential truths of the Christian faith, from our need for salvation to the grace offered through Jesus Christ. Each verse along this road is a stepping stone, leading us closer to comprehending the depth of God's love and the transformative power of faith.

Following the Roman Road, we delve into the Four Spiritual Laws, a concise yet profound framework that outlines the fundamental principles of the Gospel. These laws provide clarity and insight into the nature of our relationship with God, our condition as humans, and the redemptive work of Jesus Christ. They are the guiding principles that lead to a deeper, more meaningful understanding of our faith and how we can live it out.

This chapter is designed for both reflection and understanding. It invites readers to ponder and internalize the profound truths of the Christian faith. Whether you are a long-time believer or new to the faith, this chapter offers valuable insights into the core messages of Christianity and how they apply to our lives.

As we navigate this pathway marked out by scripture and doctrine, we do so with an open heart and mind, ready to explore, question, and understand. This journey is about connecting deeply with the fundamental truths of our faith, and how these truths shape our relationship with God and guide our daily living.

In "The Pathway Marked Out," we are on a quest for deeper spiritual understanding and enlightenment. Let us walk this path together, uncovering the richness of the Roman Road and the clarity of the Four Spiritual Laws, as we seek to deepen our faith and understanding of the Christian Journey.

What is the Roman Road to Salvation?

As we embark on chapter seven, "The Pathway Marked Out," we are about to explore one of the most foundational and illuminating paths in Christian doctrine—the Roman Road to Salvation. This journey through the Roman Road is not just a theological exploration; it is a pathway illuminated by Scripture, leading us to a deeper understanding of salvation and our personal relationship with God.

Discovering the Roman Road

The Roman Road to Salvation is a series of verses from the Apostles Paul's letter to the Romans that collectively present a clear and concise pathway to the salvation. This Road is more than a mere collection of verses; it's a spiritual journey that succinctly outlines the core principles of the Christian faith and the steps to salvation.

The Stages of the Journey

Each verse along the Roman Road serves as a guidepost, marking significant stages in the journey of faith. From acknowledging our human condition and the need for salvation to embracing the grace offered through Jesus Christ, the Roman Road lays out a clear path to understanding and accepting the gift of salvation.

A Road for All

What makes the Roman Road so compelling is its universality and simplicity. It is a journey that speaks to all, regardless of background, culture, or personal history. It articulates fundamental truths in a way that is accessible and relatable, making it a powerful tool for both personal reflection and evangelism.

Exploring the Scriptures

As we delve into this topic, we will explore each key verse along the Roman Road, unpacking its meaning and significance. We will discover how these verses collectively form a coherent and profound narrative of salvation—from recognition of our need for a Savior to the assurance of eternal life through Christ.

In "What is the Roman Road to Salvation?" we are not just learning about a series of verses; we are embarking on a journey that gets to the heart of the Christian message. It's a pathway that has guided countless individuals to a deeper understanding of their faith and has been a cornerstone in the Christian journey.

Ivy's Journey Along the Roman Road

Ivy, a 28-year-old elementary school teacher in Chicago, had always been a spiritual seeker, drifting among various beliefs and philosophies without ever truly finding a home. Raised in a culturally religious family that seldom discussed the depth of Christian faith, Ivy's understanding of Christianity was more tradition than conviction.

Having witnessed the impact of various hardships on her family and community, Ivy found herself yearning for something more concrete and fulfilling. The vague spiritualities she had dabbled in left her with more questions than answers, creating an underlying current of restlessness and uncertainty.

During a community book club meeting, a new member, who had recently embraced Christianity, mentioned the "Roman Road to Salvation" while discussing religious narratives. Intrigued, Ivy asked to learn more, and the club member shared a list of verses from the book of Romans, explaining how these scriptures outline the path to a meaningful faith and assurance of salvation.

Ivy's Exploration:

1. **Intellectual Curiosity:** Ivy began her journey on the Roman Road with intellectual curiosity, starting with Romans 3:23, "For all have sinned and fall short of the glory of God." This verse struck a chord, challenging her to confront her own imperfections and the universal need for grace.

2. **Emotional Connection:** As she progressed to Romans 5:8, "But God demonstrates His own love for us in this: While we were still sinners, Christ died for us," Ivy felt an emotional stir. This concept of unconditional love and sacrifice spoke to her deeply, filling a void she had long felt in her spiritual life.

3. **Decision Point:** Reaching Romans 10:9, "If you declare with your mouth, 'Jesus is Lord,' and believe in your heart that God raised him from the dead, you will be saved," Ivy found herself at a crossroads. The clarity and simplicity of the step appealed to her intellect and emotions alike, prompting her to make a personal decision.

4. **Transformation:** The culmination of Ivy's journey along the Roman Road was a profound personal transformation. She began to integrate her new faith into her daily life, finding peace and purpose that had previously eluded her. Her decision to embrace the teachings of the Roman Road led to a revitalized spirit and a new commitment to living out her beliefs.

Ivy's story is a testament to the power of the Roman Road to reach individuals at their point of need, offering a clear and accessible path to salvation that resonates on intellectual, emotional, and spiritual levels. Her journey from curiosity to conviction illustrates how this ancient path continues to guide seekers to profound truths and life-changing faith.

What are the Four Spiritual Laws?

As we journey further into chapter seven, we encounter a cornerstone of evangelical Christian belief—the Four Spiritual Laws. These laws present a clear and structured way to understand our relationship with God, distilled into four fundamental truths supported by Scripture. They serve as guideposts, leading us toward a deeper comprehension of salvation and our place in God's plan.

Law One: God's Love and Plan

The first law states, "God loves you and offers a wonderful plan for your life." This truth is foundational to Christian belief and is beautifully encapsulated in John 3:16, "For God so loved the world that He gave His one and only Son, that whoever believes in Him shall not perish but have eternal life." This verse affirms God's immense love for us and His desire for us to have a life filled with purpose and meaning.

Law Two: Humanity's Problem—Sin

The second law addresses the problem that separates us from God: "Humanity is tainted by sin and is therefore separated from God." Romans 3:23 supports this law: "For all have sinned and fall short of the glory of God." This verse highlights the universal nature of sin and its impact on our spiritual relationship with God.

Law Three: Jesus Christ—The Only Answer

The third law introduces the solution to this problem: "Jesus Christ is God's only provision for human sin. Through Him, you can know and experience God's love and plan for your life." Romans 5:8 declares, "But God demonstrates His own love for us in this: While we were still sinners, Christ died for us." This verse beautifully illustrates how Jesus' sacrifice bridges the gap caused by our sin.

Law Four: Our response—The Need to Receive Christ

Finally, the fourth law calls for personal response: "We must individually receive Jesus Christ as Savior and Lord; then we can know and experience God's love and plan for our lives." John 1:12 provides clarity: "Yet to all who did receive Him, to those who believed in His name, He gave the right to become children of God." This verse emphasizes the need for personal acceptance of Jesus Christ as our Savior.

The Four Spiritual Laws serve as a simple yet profound roadmap to understanding our relationship with God. They encapsulate the essence of the Gospel message, guiding us from recognizing our need for a Savior to embracing the salvation offered through Jesus Christ.

In exploring "What are the Four Spiritual Laws?" we gain not only a deeper understanding of these principles but also a framework for how we can apply them to our lives. It's a journey that takes us to the heart of Christian faith, offering clarity and direction for our spiritual path.

Gabriel's Discovery of the Four Spiritual Laws

Gabriel, a 34-year-old software developer from San Diego, had always approached life with a logical and methodical mindset. Raised in a secular household, his interactions with spirituality were sparse and skeptical. However, a challenging period in his personal life led him to search for deeper meaning and purpose beyond the tangible world he knew so well.

Struggling with the recent loss of a close family member, Gabriel found himself grappling with existential questions that his secular worldview struggled to answer. He felt a profound emptiness and a desire for something solid to anchor his life around, leading him to explore various spiritual paths without much conviction.

During a casual conversation at a coffee shop, a friend mentioned the Four Spiritual Laws, a concept Gabriel had never encountered. Intrigued by the structured approach to spirituality, he decided to delve deeper, requesting a copy of a pamphlet detailing these laws from his friend.

Gabriel's Exploration of Each Law:

1. **Intellectual Engagement:** As Gabriel read about the first law, "God loves you and offers a wonderful plan for your life," he was initially skeptical. However, the clear and straightforward explanation, backed by the scriptural verse John 3:16, appealed to his logical side, prompting him to consider the implications of a life designed with purpose.

2. **Emotional Resonance:** The second law, highlighting humanity's separation from God due to sin (Romans 3:23), struck an emotional chord. Gabriel realized his feelings of emptiness could be manifestations of this separation. This realization began to shift his perspective from indifference to curiosity about the role of spirituality in personal fulfillment.

3. **Decision-Making Process:** Upon encountering the third law, which presents Jesus Christ as the solution to humanity's sin through His sacrifice (Romans 5:8), Gabriel faced a critical decision point. This law challenged him to consider accepting a belief system that offered redemption and hope, concepts that had become increasingly relevant in his life.

4. **Commitment and Transformation:** The fourth law required a personal response, as detailed in John 1:12. Making the decision to accept Jesus Christ as his Savior was both a culmination of his intellectual and emotional journey and a starting point for a new spiritual path.

Gabriel's engagement with the Four Spiritual Laws marked a significant transformation in his life. He found not only answers to his existential queries but also a new community within a local church, where he deepened his understanding and connection. This journey from skepticism to faith transformed Gabriel, offering him a newfound sense of peace and purpose.

His story highlights how the Four Spiritual Laws can serve as a compelling framework for those seeking clarity about their spiritual path, effectively addressing the intellectual, emotional, and volitional aspects of their journey toward faith.

Living the Truths: Applying the Roman Road and Spiritual Laws in Daily Life

After exploring the Roman Road and the Four Spiritual Laws, it's crucial to understand how these theological concepts translate into everyday Christian practice. This section, "Living the Truths," provides practical advice and examples of how believers can apply these foundational teachings in their daily interactions, decisions, and spiritual growth.

Integrating the Teachings into Daily Life

This part of the chapter delves into how the truths from the Roman Road and the Four Spiritual Laws can influence and guide daily decisions and behaviors. It offers insight into integrating these spiritual principles into everyday actions, such as:

- **Forgiveness and Reconciliation:** Drawing from the Roman Road's emphasis on grace, this subsection can discuss how understanding and accepting God's grace compels believers to forgive and seek reconciliation with others.

- **Evangelism and Witnessing:** Utilizing the clarity provided by the Four Spiritual Laws, this portion can explore effective ways to share the Gospel, emphasizing the importance of personal testimony and relational evangelism.

Challenges and Encouragements

Here, the discussion can focus on the common challenges believers face when trying to live out their faith according to these doctrines and provide biblical encouragement for overcoming these obstacles. It can include scriptural references that offer strength and guidance for persisting in faith despite trials and doubts.

Community and Fellowship

This approach can emphasize the importance of Christian community in reinforcing the teachings of the Roman Road and the Four Spiritual Laws. It can illustrate how fellowship with other believers helps to deepen understanding of these truths and provides support in living them out.

Testimonies of Transformation

Collecting real-life stories and testimonies from individuals whose lives have been transformed by applying these biblical truths can powerfully demonstrate their practical impact. This part of the section can serve as a motivational tool, showing the tangible changes that occur when believers truly live according to the principles outlined in the Roman Road and the Four Spiritual Laws.

Logan's Journey Through Faith and Community

Logan, a 35-year-old community organizer from Atlanta, discovered a deeper connection to his faith through the Roman Road and the Four Spiritual Laws during a challenging period in his personal and professional life. His journey reflects a powerful integration of these teachings into daily living.

Logan had always struggled with the concepts of forgiveness and reconciliation, both in his family life and within the communities he served. His parents had separated when he was young, leaving him with unresolved anger and a sense of abandonment that he carried into adulthood.

The pivotal moment came during a community workshop aimed at reducing neighborhood violence, where Logan used the Four Spiritual Laws as a framework to address underlying issues of resentment and mistrust. His approach, rooted in his newfound understanding of grace and redemption, led to a breakthrough moment with a local gang leader, sparking a wider movement of reconciliation within the community.

Daily Application of Theological Concepts:

1. **Forgiveness and Reconciliation:** Inspired by the Roman Road's focus on grace, Logan began to actively seek reconciliation with his estranged father. Their journey towards forgiveness transformed Logan's approach to

community work, emphasizing empathy and understanding over judgment.

2. **Evangelism and Witnessing:** Logan utilized the clarity of the Four Spiritual Laws to facilitate open discussions about faith and morality in his community groups. His ability to relate these laws to everyday struggles helped many in his community find a personal connection to the Gospel, enhancing their engagement and commitment to change.

3. **Challenges and Encouragements:** Logan faced significant resistance, both internally from his doubts and externally from those skeptical of mixing faith with community work. He found encouragement in Scriptures like Philippians 4:13, "I can do all things through Christ who strengthens me," which he shared frequently to inspire persistence and resilience.

4. **Community and Fellowship:** The importance of community was never clearer to Logan than when seeing former adversaries come together in fellowship. This unity was further deepened during group studies of the Roman Road and the Four Spiritual Laws, fostering a shared understanding and mutual respect.

5. **Testimonies of Transformation:** At a community forum, Logan shared his personal testimony, highlighting his journey towards forgiveness and how it was mirrored in his professional efforts to heal and unite his neighborhood. His story, grounded in the principles of the

Roman Road and the Four Spiritual Laws, served as a beacon of hope and a practical example of living faith in action.

Logan's story is a testament to the profound impact that living out the truths of the Roman Road and the Four Spiritual Laws can have on a personal and community level. His journey from personal strife to community leader exemplifies how deeply faith can influence not just individual lives but also broader societal healing and unity.

———

Conclusion

As we draw chapter seven, "The Pathway Marked Out," to a close, we reflect on the enlightening journey we've taken through the Roman Road and the Four Spiritual Laws. This chapter has been more than a mere exploration of biblical verses and evangelical principles; it has been a profound journey into the heart of our faith, illuminating the pathway to salvation and a deeper understanding of our relationship with God.

Our walk along the Roman Road has revealed the depth and richness of Paul's teachings. Through this journey, we've gained insights into the fundamental truths of sin, grace, and salvation. Each verse on this road has guided us to a clearer understanding of our need for a Savior and God's incredible provision through Jesus Christ.

Delving into the Four Spiritual Laws, we've unpacked the simplicity and clarity of the Gospel message. These laws have provided us with a structured framework to understand our position before God, the profound problem of sin, the unmatched solution through Christ, and the invitation for a personal response. This exploration has highlighted the importance of each law in guiding us towards a meaningful and transformative faith.

This chapter has been an invitation to personal reflection and growth. It has encouraged us to consider where we stand on this pathway and how we respond to the truths presented in the Gospel. Whether we are at the beginning of our faith journey or further along the road, the insights gained here are invaluable in deepening our understanding and relationship with God.

As we conclude this chapter, let us carry forward the lessons learned. May the Roman Road and the Four Spiritual Laws serve as continual guides in our spiritual journey, providing clarity, direction, and inspiration. Let these principles enrich our daily walk with Christ, influencing how we live, how we share our faith, and how we grow in our understanding of God's love and salvation.

In "The Pathway Marked Out," we have journeyed through foundational teachings that are essential for every believer. As we turn the page, let us do so with renewed commitment to our faith, equipped with a deeper understanding and appreciation for the profound journey of salvation.

The Verdict of Faith: Are You Truly Following Christ?

"Then he said to them all: 'Whoever wants to be my disciple must deny themselves and take up their cross daily and follow me'."
—LUKE 9:23 NIV

In Chapter eight, "The Verdict of Faith," we embark on a soul-searching journey to confront and explore one of the most essential questions in the Christian life: Are we truly following Christ? This chapter isn't just an exploration; it's a mirror held up to our faith, inviting us to examine our relationship with Christ with honesty and depth.

We begin by diving into the heart of what it means to be a 'real' Christian. This quest takes us beyond superficial labels and societal perceptions, delving into the core of Christian identity. It's an exploration that intertwines Scripture with self-reflection, challenging us to evaluate whether our lives truly reflect Christ's teachings and love.

Following this, we delve into the profound topic of "7 Things God Wants To Do for You." This segment is a heartwarming reminder of the incredible ways God wishes to work in and through our lives. From His desire to provide and guide to His promise of eternal life, we explore the breadth and depth of God's benevolent intentions for us, as revealed through His word.

This chapter is an invitation to authenticity in our faith journey. It calls us to assess our walk with Christ not just in terms of external observance but through the deeper metrics of spiritual transformation, obedience, and love. It's a call to align our hearts, minds, and actions with the teachings of Jesus, living out our faith with integrity and purpose.

As we journey through "The Verdict of Faith," we are encouraged to reflect on our personal commitment to Christ. This chapter aims to inspire a renewed dedication to living a life that truly follows Christ, one that is marked by genuine faith, steadfast love, and unwavering commitment to His path.

In embarking on this chapter, let us approach with open hearts and minds, ready to engage in an honest evaluation of our faith and to embrace the transformative journey of truly following Christ.

What is a Real Christian?

As we embark on chapter eight, "The Verdict of Faith," we engage in one of the most fundamental and introspective discussions in the Christian journey—understanding what it truly means to be a 'real' Christian. This exploration is not just an academic exercise; it's a soul-searching quest that delves into the essence of our faith, challenging us to reflect on our own walk with Christ.

The Hallmark of Faith

At the heart of being a real Christian is the hallmark of faith. But this faith is not mere belief in the existence of God or acknowledgment of Christ's historical reality. James 2:19 reminds us that even the demons believe in God's existence, yet their knowledge does not lead to salvation. True Christian faith is transformative, marked by a deep trust in Jesus Christ as Lord and Savior and a commitment to following His teachings.

Living Out the Teachings of Christ

Being a real Christian extends beyond faith; it encompasses living out the teachings of Christ. Jesus Himself outlined the essence of this lifestyle in Matthew 7:21, where He declared, "Not everyone who says to me, 'Lord, Lord,' will enter the kingdom of heaven, but only the one who does the will of my Father who is in heaven." This verse underscores the importance of obedience and action in the Christian life.

The Fruits of the Spirit

A real Christian is also identified by the fruits of the Spirit, as listed in Galatians 5:22–23—love, joy, peace, forbearance, kindness, goodness, faithfulness, gentleness, and self-control. These qualities are not just ideals to strive for; they are the natural byproduct of a life deeply connected to Christ.

Love: The Defining Characteristic

The defining characteristic of a real Christian is love. John 13:35 succinctly states, "By this everyone will know that you are my disciples, if you love one another." This love is not just an emotion but an action—it's a love that serves, forgives, and embraces others, reflecting the love that Christ has shown to us.

A Continuous Journey

Understanding what it means to be a real Christian is not a destination; it's a continuous journey. It involves daily decisions to follow Christ, to embody His teachings, and to reflect His love in our interactions with the world.

In "What is a Real Christian?" We seek not just to define a term but to understand a way of life. This chapter invites us to examine our own lives in light of the teachings of Christ, to assess whether we are truly living as His followers, and to recommit ourselves to the path He has set before us.

———

Hazel's Journey to Living Faith

Hazel, a 34-year-old elementary school teacher, embodies the spirit of community and care. Every day, she wears a small silver cross around her neck, a gift from her mother, symbolizing her faith. But despite this token, she often wonders what it truly means to be a real Christian, especially in the trying times of her profession.

Lately, Hazel has found herself wrestling with doubts and frustrations, feeling disconnected from her faith. She questions the depth of her beliefs and struggles with the harsh realities that her students face, which often seem at odds with the loving world her faith promises.

It was during a particularly challenging parent-teacher conference that Hazel's understanding shifted. Facing an irate parent upset over their child's performance, Hazel felt an overwhelming sense of calm. Instead of responding with defensiveness or frustration, she found herself speaking with unexpected kindness and patience, driven by a deeper empathy. This was not just professional decorum but a spontaneous expression of genuine care and understanding— the fruits of the Spirit in action.

As the parent stormed out, leaving behind a quieter, reflective atmosphere, Hazel realized the true essence of her faith. It wasn't just about wearing her cross or attending church; it was about embodying Christ's teachings in moments of trial. This experience led her to delve deeper into her spiritual journey, engaging more actively with her community and church, and finding that her faith became more vibrant and connected, not only enriching her life but also empowering her to impact those around her positively.

In this chapter, "The Verdict of Faith," Hazel's story serves as a beacon for readers, illustrating that being a real Christian is about living a transformative faith through actions that echo Christ's love and teachings. This realization renews her commitment to her faith journey, proving that real Christianity is lived out in the day-to-day moments of grace and kindness.

---

7 Things God Wants To Do for You

In this segment of chapter eight, we explore the gracious and loving intentions God has for each of us. "7 Things God Wants To Do for You" is more than just a list; it's a revelation of God's heart and desires for His children, as expressed through Scripture. Each item on this list is a reminder of God's active presence and benevolence in our lives.

1. God Wants to Give You Salvation

First and foremost, God desires to grant you salvation. Ephesians 2:8 says, "For it is by grace you have been saved, through faith—and this is not from yourselves, it is the gift of God." This verse highlights that salvation is a gift from God, given freely through His grace, and is the foundation of our relationship with Him.

2. God Desires to Give You Peace

God wants to bless you with peace. In John 14:27, Jesus said, "Peace, I leave with you; my peace I give you. I do not give to you as the world gives. Do not let your hearts be troubled and do not be afraid." This peace surpasses all understanding and is a testament to the comfort and assurance we find in God.

3. God Wants to Provide for You

God's desire is also to provide for your needs. Philippians 4:19 assures us of this: "And my God will meet all your needs according to the riches of His glory in Jesus Christ." This promise speaks to God's provision, assuring us that He is attentive to our needs.

4. God Seeks to Guide You

God wants to be your guide. Psalm 32:8 declares, "I will instruct you and teach you in the way you should go; I will counsel you with my loving eye on you." God's guidance is a precious gift, leading us along the best path for our lives.

5. God Wishes to Empower You

Empowerment is another gift God wants to give. In 2 Timothy 1:7, we read, "For the Spirit God gave us does not make us timid, but gives us power, love and self-discipline." This empowerment enables us to live boldly, love freely, and maintain self-discipline.

6. God Desires to Heal and Restore You

God longs to bring healing and restoration. Psalm 147:3 says, "He heals the brokenhearted and binds up their wounds." This verse speaks to God's concern for our emotional and physical well-being and His ability to bring healing and restoration.

7. God Wants to Give You Eternal Life

Finally, God wants to grant you eternal life. John 3:16, one of the most famous verses in the Bible, affirms this: "For God so loved the world that He gave His one and only Son, that whoever believes in Him shall not perish but have eternal life." This is the ultimate expression of God's love and desire for us.

Each of these seven things reflects the depth of God's love and His commitment to our well-being. In exploring "7 Things God Wants To Do for You," we are reminded of the many ways God shows His love and care for us, encouraging us to trust in His plans and promises.

─────

Jackson's Discovery of Divine Support

Jackson, a 45-year-old community center director, devotes his life to helping others. His job is demanding and often leaves him feeling depleted both emotionally and spiritually. He wears a well-worn leather bracelet with the inscription "Faith Over Fear," a constant reminder of his need to rely on something greater than himself.

Despite his strong exterior, Jackson battles with a deep-seated anxiety about the future and the effectiveness of his work. He often lies awake at night, questioning if his efforts are making any real difference in the challenging neighborhood he serves.

The turning point came one quiet evening at the community center after everyone had left. Jackson sat reviewing grant applications and felt overwhelmed by the enormity of the needs and the scarcity of resources. In that moment of quiet desperation, he stumbled upon a passage in a devotional book open on his desk: "And my God will meet all your needs according to the riches of his glory in Jesus Christ" (Philippians 4:19). It was as if the verse was speaking directly to him, offering not just spiritual but practical reassurance.

This moment of discovery was profound. Jackson felt a sudden, overwhelming peace envelop him; the kind promised in John 14:27. This peace reassured him that he was not alone in his mission. The following weeks brought unexpected donations and support, reinforcing his faith in God's provision. He also found new strength and courage, echoing 2 Timothy 1:7, allowing him to tackle challenges with renewed vigor and hope.

Through these experiences, Jackson realized that the list of what God wants to do for him was not just abstract promises but tangible realities. He saw firsthand how God sought to guide, provide for, and empower him, leading to both personal and community transformation. Jackson's story illustrates the living reality of God's active benevolence, reminding us all that the divine desires outlined in Scripture are as practical as they are profound, aiming to uplift and sustain us in every aspect of life.

Overcoming Obstacles: Staying True to Christ in Trials

This section delves into the common challenges that believers may face as they strive to live according to Christ's teachings. It provides biblical guidance on how to overcome these obstacles and remain steadfast in faith, even under pressure or in the face of adversity.

Recognizing and Overcoming Spiritual Challenges

This part of the chapter identifies specific spiritual challenges such as doubt, worldly distractions, or persecution. It offers scriptural advice on how to navigate these issues based on the teachings of Jesus and the experiences of early Christians as documented in the New Testament.

Examples from Scripture

Incorporating examples from the Bible, such as the perseverance of Job, Paul's trials, or Peter's journey from denial to proclamation, illustrates how challenges were overcome by faith and serve as models for personal application.

Practical Steps to Maintain Faith

Offering practical advice on maintaining one's faith during difficult times could be extremely beneficial. This might include maintaining a regular prayer life, engaging in Bible study, seeking fellowship with other believers, and finding ways to serve others despite personal struggles.

Testimonies of Modern Believers

Sharing testimonies from contemporary Christians who have faced and overcome significant trials while remaining faithful to their Christian walk can provide inspiration and concrete examples of how the principles discussed can be applied in today's world.

Eliza's Journey Through Trials to Triumph

Eliza, a 38-year-old nurse in an oncology ward, confronts daily the stark realities of life and death. Known for her compassionate care, she wears a small, engraved pendant with the word "Hope" that her patients often notice and comment on. Despite her strong faith, the relentless pressure and emotional toll of her job sometimes shake the very foundations of her beliefs.

Eliza grapples with profound questions about suffering and divine purpose, especially after particularly grueling days. These challenges to her faith are compounded by the personal grief of recently losing her mother to the very illness she fights against every day.

One evening, after a particularly tough day when a young patient passed away, Eliza found herself in the hospital's small chapel, questioning everything. As tears streamed down her face, she opened a Bible to a random page, desperately seeking some solace or sign. Her eyes fell on James 1:12, "Blessed is the one who perseveres under trial because, having stood the test, that person will receive the crown of life that the Lord has promised to those who love him." This scripture spoke directly to her heart, reigniting her faith and reinforcing her resolve to remain steadfast.

This scripture became a turning point for Eliza. She began to integrate more deliberate spiritual practices into her daily routine, such as morning prayers and weekly Bible study sessions. She also started a support group at the hospital for staff dealing with grief and loss, providing a space for healing and mutual encouragement.

Eliza's story of overcoming spiritual challenges illustrates the profound impact of staying true to Christ in trials. Her journey shows that, despite the pressures and adversities of life, maintaining a connection to one's faith can offer not only personal strength but also extend hope and healing to others. Eliza's renewed faith and her practical steps to engage more deeply with her spiritual life transformed her personal trials into a testimony of perseverance and divine faithfulness, inspiring her colleagues and patients alike.

Conclusion

As we draw chapter eight, "The Verdict of Faith," to a close, we stand at a moment of reflection and deep contemplation. This chapter has been a profound journey through the heart of what it means to truly follow Christ. We've explored the essence of a genuine Christian life and discovered the beautiful intentions God has for each of us.

Our exploration began with delving into the question, "What is a Real Christian?" We've been challenged to look beyond the surface, to examine our hearts and lives against the teachings and example of Jesus. This journey has reminded us that being a Christian is more than a label; it's a way of life, a transformation that touches every aspect of our existence.

In discovering the "7 Things God Wants To Do for You," we've seen the depth of God's love and the breadth of His plans for us. From offering salvation and peace to guiding, empowering, and ultimately granting eternal life, we have been reminded of the numerous ways God manifests His love and care in our lives.

As we conclude this chapter, let us carry forward the insights and lessons learned. May the understanding of what it truly means to be a Christian influence our daily choices and actions. Let us embrace the gifts and plans God has for us, trusting in His guidance and providence.

Let this chapter be a call to authentic Christian living. May we strive to reflect Christ in our thoughts, words, and deeds. Let us be beacons of His love and grace, living testimonies of the transformative power of faith.

In "The Verdict of Faith," we have not just sought answer; we have embarked on a journey of spiritual growth and renewal. As we turn the page from this chapter, let us do so with a renewed commitment to live out our faith with sincerity, courage, and unwavering devotion to Christ.

The Assurance of Trial: Tests and Confirmations of a Saved Soul Faith

"Blessed is the one who perseveres under trial because, having stood the test, that person will receive the crown of life that the Lord has promised to those who love Him." —JAMES 1:12 NIV

In chapter nine, "The Assurance of Trial," please step into a realm of introspection and affirmation, where we seek to understand and confirm the authenticity of our salvation. This chapter is not merely an academic exercise; it's a spiritual expedition that delves deep into the heart of what it means to possess a saved soul. It's about examining the evidence of our faith and understanding the signs that indicate a genuine relationship with Christ.

We begin by addressing one of the most profound concerns of any believer: the assurance of salvation. This is a journey that combines scriptural wisdom with personal introspection, guiding us through confirmations and warnings that help us discern the true state of our salvation. It's an exploration that encourages us to look within, to assess our relationship with God, and to seek his confirmation in our lives.

Following this, we explore "Testing the Fruits: Signs of a Living Faith." Here, we engage in an examination of the tangible evidence of a living and active faith. Drawing from biblical teachings, we learn to identify the fruits of the spirit in our lives—love, joy, peace, patience, kindness, goodness, faithfulness, gentleness, and self-control. This section is not just about recognition; it's about cultivation—nurturing these fruits in our daily walk with Christ.

This chapter is a journey of confirmation. It invites us to affirm our faith, to understand the evidences of a life transformed by Christ, and to stand confidently in the assurance of our salvation. It's a chapter that challenges us to be honest with ourselves, to confront our doubts, and to seek the truth with a sincere heart.

As we embark on "The Assurance of Trial," let us do so with open hearts and minds. This chapter calls us to embrace the trial, not as a judgment, but as an opportunity for growth, reassurance, and a deeper connection with God. It's a path that leads to greater clarity, stronger faith, and a more profound understanding of our spiritual journey.

In embarking on this chapter, may we find the assurance we seek and the confirmation we need to continue our walk and faith, knowing that our journey is guided by His truth and love.

The Assurance of Salvation: Confirmations and Warnings

In chapter nine, "The Assurance of Trial," we venture into the vital yet often challenging terrain of understanding and confirming the assurance of salvation. This is a journey that intertwines scriptural wisdom with introspective examination, guiding us to discern the true state of our salvation and to recognize the signs and warnings along the way.

The Testimony of Scripture

Our exploration begins with the testimony of scripture, which offers both assurances and cautions regarding salvation. 1 John 5:13 declares, "I write these things to you who believe in the name of the Son of God so that you may know that you have eternal life." This verse is a beacon of assurance, affirming that belief in Jesus Christ is the foundation of our salvation.

Confirmations of a Saved Soul

At the same time, scripture provides warnings to guard against complacency. Matthew 7:21–23 cautions, "Not everyone who says to me, 'Lord, Lord' will enter the kingdom of heaven, but only the one who does the will of My Father who is in heaven." This passage urges us to examine the authenticity of our faith, ensuring that our declaration of Christ as Lord is matched by a life that seeks to do God's will.

The Role of Faith and Works

In this chapter, we also explore the role of faith and works in the assurance of salvation. James 2:17 reminds us, "In the same way, faith by itself, if it is not accomplished by action, is dead." This first highlights that genuine faith is evidenced by the works it produces, serving as a confirmation of our commitment to Christ.

Navigating Doubts and Fears

Lastly, we address the experience of doubts and fears that may arise in our spiritual journey. Doubts do not necessarily negate the assurance of salvation; rather, they can be an opportunity for growth and deeper understanding. Philippians 1:6 offers comfort, stating, "being confident of this, that he who began a good work in you will carry it on to completion until the day of Christ Jesus."

"The Assurance of Salvation: Confirmations and Warnings" is a comprehensive exploration of how we can find assurance in our faith while remaining vigilant against complacency. It's a journey that invites us to reflect deeply on our spiritual state and seek continual growth in our relationship with Christ.

Aiden's Journey to Assurance

Aiden, a 50-year-old small business owner, has always prided himself on his self-reliance and practical approach to life. He wears a well-worn watch—a gift from his father, reminding him of the value of time and diligence. Despite his outward success, Aiden wrestles with internal doubts about his spiritual life, particularly concerning the assurance of his salvation.

Aiden's doubts are magnified by the pressures of his business and the personal losses he has recently endured, leading him to question the depth and authenticity of his faith. He often lies awake at night, pondering if his belief is genuine or merely a facade influenced by his community and family expectations.

The turning point came on a Sunday morning when Aiden, sitting alone in the back pew of his church, listened to a sermon on 1 John 5:13. The message that belief in Jesus Christ assures us of eternal life struck a chord deep within him. It was a profound moment of clarity, as if the verse was speaking directly to his lingering uncertainties.

This scripture initiated a transformative journey for Aiden. He began to actively seek confirmations of his faith through his actions, not just in his business dealings but also in how he interacted with his community. He volunteered more, offered support to struggling neighbors, and became a mentor to young entrepreneurs, aligning his actions with the teachings of Christ.

Aiden's story of grappling with the assurance of salvation and finding confirmation through scripture and deeds illustrates a compelling narrative of spiritual growth. His journey underscores that while doubts may arise, they serve as a catalyst for deeper engagement with faith. Through his renewed commitment, Aiden experiences a sense of peace and assurance, affirming that his salvation is not just a hope but a present reality, energizing him to live a life that reflects the true spirit of his beliefs.

Testing the Fruits: Signs of a Living Faith

In this part of chapter nine, we turn our focus to "Testing the Fruits," an explanation of the visible signs and evidences of a living and active faith. This section is not just an examination; it's a journey into understanding how the fruits of our faith manifest in our lives, as affirmed by Scripture.

The Biblical Basis for Fruitful Living

The concept of testing the fruits of our faith is deeply rooted in Scripture. Matthew 7:16–20 offers clear guidance, with Jesus teaching, "By their fruit you will recognize them . . . Every good tree bears good fruit, but a bad tree bears bad fruit." This passage lays the foundation for understanding that a living faith is identifiable by the qualities and actions it produces.

Identifying the Fruits of the Spirit

Galatians 5:22–23 provides a definitive list of the fruits of the Spirit: "But the fruit of the Spirit is love, joy, peace, forbearance, kindness, goodness, faithfulness, gentleness, and self-control." These attributes are not just ideals to aspire to; they are tangible indicators of the Spirit's work within us. They are the signs that our faith is not static but dynamic and transformative.

Love: The Foremost Fruit

Among these fruits, love holds a place of preeminence. 1 Corinthians 13:13 asserts, "And now these three remain: faith, hope, and love. But the greatest of these is love." This emphasis on love highlights its central role in our Christian walk. It is through our capacity to love—God, others, and ourselves—that the authenticity of our faith is most powerfully demonstrated.

The Fruits in Action

Living faith is faith in action. James 2:18 challenges believers with the assertions, "Show me your faith without deeds, and I will show you my faith by my deeds." This call to action reminds us that our faith should be evident in how we live our lives, how we interact with others, and how we serve our communities.

Continual Growth and Nurturing

Testing the fruits of our faith is not a one-time assessment; it's an ongoing process of growth and nurturing. Just as a gardener tends to the garden, we too must nurture our spiritual lives, ensuring that the seeds of faith planted within us grow and flourish.

In "Testing the Fruits: Signs of a Living Faith," we are invited to reflect on the visible manifestations of our faith. This exploration encourages us to examine our lives, to identify the fruits of our faith, and to strive continually for spiritual growth and maturity.

Faith's Journey to Nurturing Faith

Faith, a 42-year-old landscape architect, harmonizes her love for nature with her spiritual journey. Known for her serene demeanor and thoughtful presence, she wears a bracelet of intertwined vines, symbolizing growth and connection. Despite her professional success, Faith seeks deeper signs of spiritual maturity in her life, reflecting on how her faith manifests in tangible ways.

Faith often feels the weight of superficiality in her social circles, which makes her question the depth and authenticity of her own faith. She longs to see real, tangible evidence of the Spirit's work in her life, beyond the surface-level interactions and achievements.

The turning point came during a community gardening project. While teaching a group of young volunteers about the importance of pruning for healthier plant growth, Faith had an epiphany about her own spiritual fruits. She realized that, like the plants she tended, her spiritual life needed regular nurturing and sometimes pruning to truly flourish.

This realization sparked a transformation in Faith's approach to her faith. She began to actively engage with her community, not just as a leader but as a participant, seeking to embody the fruits of the Spirit in her daily interactions. Her efforts to demonstrate love, joy, peace, and kindness became more intentional. Faith also started a small group for spiritual reflection in her community, providing a space for others to explore and cultivate their faith.

Faith's story illustrates the process of "Testing the Fruits" in a practical, impactful way. Her journey from recognizing the need for genuine spiritual fruits to actively cultivating them in her life and community shows that faith is not static but grows and evolves through conscious effort and engagement. Her life becomes a testament to the dynamic and transformative nature of living faith, inspiring others to look beyond the surface and nurture the deeper spiritual fruits within themselves.

Living Out Your Salvation: Practical Steps for Daily Assurance

This section focuses on the practical aspects of embodying one's salvation in everyday life, offering guidance on how believers can continually affirm their faith through actions and lifestyle choices that reflect their commitment to Christ.

Daily Practices for Spiritual Growth

Exploring daily spiritual disciplines such as prayer, meditation on Scripture, and fellowship can be crucial. This practice provides practical advice on how to integrate these practices into daily routines to strengthen one's faith and assurance of salvation.

Overcoming Spiritual Complacency

Addressing the risk of becoming spiritually complacent, this practice teaches how to stay vigilant in one's faith journey. It could offer insights into recognizing signs of complacency and strategies for re-engaging with one's spiritual growth actively.

Community and Accountability

Highlighting the importance of community in the Christian life, this practice can explore how being part of a church or small group provides not only support but also accountability that helps maintain the health of one's spiritual life.

Testimonies of Transformed Lives

Incorporating testimonies from individuals who have experienced significant transformation through their faith can serve as powerful illustrations of living out one's salvation. These stories can inspire and provide concrete examples of how the principles discussed can be actualized.

Theo's Journey to Living Out Salvation

Theo, a 36-year-old urban planner, lives in the bustling heart of the city but strives to maintain a tranquil spirit influenced by his deep Christian faith. He carries a pocket-sized Bible and a journal, tools that guide his reflections and decisions. Despite his hectic schedule, Theo has always sought ways to make his faith a visible part of his life.

Lately, Theo has felt the pressure of urban life weighing on him, challenging his peace and testing his faith. He worries about losing touch with his spiritual side and becoming another faceless cog in the city's endless machine.

The turning point came during a particularly challenging urban development meeting, where conflicting interests threatened to derail a community project. Theo felt an internal nudge to pause and offer a silent prayer for wisdom and patience. This simple act of faith changed the atmosphere, calming his thoughts and influencing his approach to the negotiation.

Inspired by this experience, Theo decided to more intentionally integrate his faith into his daily routine. He began starting his day with 15 minutes of scripture meditation, which he found not only grounded him spiritually but also enhanced his focus and empathy throughout the day. Theo also joined a weekly faith-based community group, which provided him a platform to share his challenges and insights, reinforcing his commitment to living out his salvation.

Encouraged by his group, Theo initiated a community service project that involved his planning skills to benefit underprivileged areas. This project became a practical application of his faith, showcasing the transformative power of Christian principles in public service.

Theo's journey illustrates that living out one's salvation involves more than just personal spiritual practices; it extends into every interaction and decision. His story emphasizes that daily reaffirmation of faith through practical steps not only strengthens personal assurance of salvation but also manifests a powerful witness to the faith in the public sphere. Theo's life becomes a beacon of how consistent, small acts of faith can lead to significant spiritual and communal transformations.

Conclusion

As we conclude chapter nine, "The Assurance of Trial," we find ourselves enriched and enlightened by a journey through the heart of our faith. This chapter has not only been a quest for understanding but also a profound affirmation of our spiritual journey. We have navigated through the depths of what it means to have assurance in our salvation and have examined the fruits that evidence a living faith.

Our exploration began with "The Assurance of Salvation: Confirmations and Warnings," where we engaged with the essential truths of our faith, discerning between genuine assurance and misplaced confidence. This part of our journey reminded us of the importance of grounding our assurance not just an emotional experiences, but in the truth of God's Word and the transformation it brings.

In "Testing the Fruits: Signs of a Living Faith," we delved into the tangible manifestations of our faith. We learned that the fruits of the Spirit are not just abstract virtues, but real and observable qualities in our lives. This exploration has challenged us to cultivate these fruits, nurturing a faith that is not only professed but genuinely lived out.

This chapter has been a call to continuous growth and introspection. It invites us to regularly examine our faith, to seek God's guidance in our spiritual journey, and to embrace the ongoing process of sanctification. It is a reminder that our spiritual growth is a lifelong journey, one that requires diligence, commitment, and an open heart.

As we move forward from "The Assurance of Trial," let us do so with a renewed sense of purpose and confidence in our walk with Christ. May the insights gained in this chapter serve as a compass and our continued journey of faith, guiding us toward deeper understanding, greater assurance, and a more profound relationship with God.

In closing chapter nine, we carry with us the valuable lessons learned about the assurance of our salvation and the fruits of a living faith. May this chapter be a milestone in our spiritual journey, strengthening our faith and fortifying our commitment to follow Christ wholeheartedly.

The Final Judgment: The Solemn Reality of Eternity

"For we must all appear before the judgment seat of Christ, so that each one may receive what is due for what he has done in the body, whether good or evil." —2 CORINTHIANS 5:10 NIV

Chapter ten, "The Final Judgment," brings us face to face with the solemn reality of eternity, a destination that awaits us all at the culmination of our earthly journey. This chapter is not just an exploration of eschatological doctrine; it is a profound reflection on the ultimate destination of every human soul and the lasting impact of our lives here on earth.

We begin this chapter by delving into "The Final Verdict: The Christian's Stand Before God." This is a moment of profound significance, where we are called to account for our lives. It's an exploration that intertwines Scripture with personal introspection, painting a vivid picture of what awaits us beyond the veil of this life. We are reminded that our time on earth is a preparation for this moment, and each choice we make echoes into eternity.

Following this, we venture into "Eternity's Echo: The Lasting Impact of Our Earthly Journey." The segment of the chapter is a contemplation on how our actions, words, and beliefs resonate beyond our temporal existence. It's an invitation to view our lives through the lens of eternity, understanding that what we do now has implications that stretch far beyond our time on earth.

Throughout this chapter, we navigate the delicate balance between living in the present and preparing for eternity. It's a journey that asks us to consider deeply the legacy we wish to leave and the kind of life that aligns with eternal truths.

As we explore these themes, the chapter calls us to live faithfully and purposefully, with an awareness that our life's journey is leading us to an inevitable encounter with the divine. It's a sobering reminder of the weight of our decisions and the power of our faith.

In embarking on chapter ten, "The Final Judgment," we are invited to journey through a topic of immense importance, one that demands our utmost attention and introspection. May this chapter guide us to live with a heightened sense of purpose, a deeper faith, and a clearer vision of the eternal implications of our earthly sojourn.

The Final Verdict: The Christian's Stand Before God

Chapter ten, "The Final Judgement," brings us to a profound and solemn aspect of Christian belief—the final verdict we each face as we stand before God. This chapter isn't just a theological exposition; it's a deep and personal exploration of the ultimate reality every Christian must confront. We delve into what Scripture tells us about this final judgment and what it means for believers.

The Certainty of Judgement

The Bible is clear about the certainty of judgement. Hebrews 9:27 states, "Just as people are destined to die once, and after that to face judgment." This verse sets the stage for our exploration, reminding us of the inevitability of standing before God's throne. It's a moment of accountability that every soul must face, a time when our lives and choices are weighed in divine balance.

The Basis of Judgement

What will be the basis of the final verdict? 2 Corinthians 5:10 offers insight: "For we must all appear before the judgment seat of Christ, so that each of us may receive what is due us for the things done while in the body, whether good or bad." This passage indicates that our actions and decisions in this life hold eternal significance, underscoring the responsibility that comes with our free will.

The Grace and Mercy of God

In this solemn reality, there is also a message of hope—the grace and mercy of God. Romans 8:1 assures us, "Therefore, there is now no condemnation for those who are in Christ Jesus." For those who have accepted Christ as Savior, this final verdict is viewed through the lens of Christ's redemptive work. It's a reminder that salvation is not earned by deeds but granted through grace.

The Call to Faithful Living

Understanding the reality of the final judgment calls us to live faithfully and purposefully. It's a motivation, not a fear, but for a life reflective of our faith in Christ. Matthew 25:21 portrays the hope of every believer: "His master replied, 'Well done, good and faithful servant! You have been faithful with a few things; I will put you in charge of many things. Come and share your Master's happiness!'" This verse encapsulates the joy and fulfillment of hearing God's affirmation of our faithfulness.

Preparing for Eternity

Finally, this topic is about preparation—living our lives in a way that prepares us for eternity. It's about making choices that reflect our understanding of this eternal truth and aligning our lives with God's will.

"The Final Verdict: The Christian's Stand Before God" is a call to introspection and preparation, a reminder of the eternal significance of our earthly journey. As we navigate through this chapter, let us do so with a heart of wisdom, humility, and anticipation for the culmination of our faith journey.

Allison's Journey of
Purpose and Preparation for Eternity

Allison, a 62-year-old retired teacher, now dedicates her time to humanitarian efforts, both locally and abroad. She wears a locket containing a verse from Romans 8:1, a personal token of her faith and a reminder of God's grace. Her life reflects a long journey of faith, punctuated by moments of doubt and renewal.

As Allison ages, she contemplates more deeply the reality of eternity and the final judgment she believes all will face. This reflection brings a mix of apprehension and peace, as she evaluates her past choices and their alignment with her faith.

The turning point in Allison's reflective journey occurred during a mission trip to a remote village, where she helped build a school. One evening, under a starlit sky, she shared stories with the local community about her life's work and the motivations behind it. As she spoke, a deep sense of fulfillment washed over her, affirming that her efforts were not just acts of charity but acts of faith in preparation for her eternal journey.

This moment of clarity inspired Allison to recommit herself to living purposefully. She initiated a community outreach program in her hometown, focusing on mentoring young women. Each relationship she cultivated and each project she undertook was done with the conscious intent of preparing for her final stand before God, making every day count.

Allison's story illustrates the profound impact of recognizing and preparing for the final judgment. Her life becomes a testament to the power of living a faith-driven life, not out of fear of judgment, but out of love and gratitude for the grace she has received. Her actions echo the biblical call to be faithful stewards of the gifts God has given, ensuring that her final verdict is one of joy and divine approval.

Allison's example serves as a beacon for others, showing that the certainty of judgment can be a motivating force to live each day with purpose, integrity, and hope, making eternal preparation a daily commitment.

Eternity's Echo: The Lasting Impact of Our Earthly Journey

In this enlightening segment of chapter ten, we turn our focus to "Eternity's Echo," exploring how our lives on earth reverberate into eternity. This topic is a profound reflection on the lasting impact of our actions, choices, and faith during our earthly journey, underscored by Scriptures wisdom.

Life as a Preparation for Eternity

The Bible teaches that our time on earth is a preparation for eternity. In 2 Corinthians 4:18, we are reminded, "So we fix our eyes not on what is seen, but on what is unseen, since what is seen is temporary, but what is unseen is eternal." This verse invites us to look beyond the immediate and transient, focusing instead on eternal implications of our lives.

The Weight of Our Actions

Our actions and decisions in life carry a weight that extends beyond our earthly existence. Jesus' words in Matthew 16:27 emphasize this: "For the Son of Man is going to come in His Father's glory with His angels, and then He will reward each person according to what they have done." This passage underscores the idea that our deeds have lasting consequences and are significant in God's eternal perspective.

Love and Service: Echoes into Eternity

The acts of love and service we perform resonate into eternity. As taught in Matthew 25:40, "The King will reply, 'Truly I tell you, whatever you did for one of the least of these brothers and sisters of mine, you did for Me.'" This powerful statement illustrates how acts of kindness and compassion are not only earthly deeds but also heavenly investments.

Faith's Lasting Legacy

The legacy of faith we leave behind is another echo that carries into eternity. Hebrews 11:4 says, "By faith Abel still speaks, even though he is dead." This verse shows that the faith and testimony of believers continue to speak and impact others long after they have left this world.

Preparing for the Echo into Eternity

As we contemplate "Eternity's Echo," it becomes clear that our earthly journey is an opportunity to sow seeds that will bloom in the eternal realms. It's a call to live with purpose, intention, and a deep awareness of the lasting impact of our lives.

In "Eternity's Echo: The Lasting Impact of Our Earthly Journey," we are invited to consider how each moment, each decision, and each act of faith in our earthly life contributes to a lasting legacy that echoes into eternity. It's a profound reminder to live our lives in a way that honors God and leaves a positive, lasting impact.

This topic aims to provide a reflective and thought provoking look at how our earthly lives impact our eternal destiny, encouraging readers to live with a perspective that transcends the temporary.

Nathan's Architectural Legacy of Faith and Impact

Nathan, a 48-year-old architect, is renowned for designing buildings that not only serve practical purposes but also inspire and uplift. He carries an old compass, a symbol of guidance, always reminding him to align his work and life with his faith.

Nathan grapples with the realization that his professional achievements, while impressive, must resonate with deeper, eternal values.

Despite his professional acclaim, Nathan feels an undercurrent of restlessness, questioning whether his contributions are merely temporal or if they indeed echo into eternity. This internal conflict challenges him to assess the lasting impact of his creations and his life.

The pivotal moment for Nathan occurred during the unveiling of a community center he designed, intended to serve the underprivileged. During the ceremony, an elderly woman approached him, expressing how the center's welcoming space brought her profound peace and a sense of community. Her words struck a chord with Nathan, illuminating the tangible impact of his work beyond mere architecture.

Inspired by this interaction, Nathan shifted his focus towards projects that prioritize sustainability, community, and spiritual upliftment. He also began volunteering his skills to non-profit organizations, aiming to create spaces that serve as refuges of hope and gateways to growth, ensuring his architectural legacy would have lasting significance.

Nathan's journey illustrates how one's earthly profession can be a powerful conduit for eternal impact. His story exemplifies the essence of "Eternity's Echo," showing that our daily decisions and professional endeavors can indeed reverberate into eternity when aligned with God's purposes. Nathan learns to see his work as a ministry, an opportunity to sow seeds of faith, community, and beauty that will flourish long after he is gone.

Through his transformed approach, Nathan not only changes the skyline but also the lives beneath it, embodying the profound belief that our lives on earth are preparation for eternity. His actions become a resonant echo into the unseen, a lasting legacy of faith and intentionality.

―――――

Reckoning with Divine Justice

In this section, we delve into the profound and complex topic of divine justice, examining how God's righteousness and mercy interplay in the final judgment. This exploration will confront the reality of God's justice, which is both fair and absolute, and consider how this understanding influences our perspective on sin and redemption.

Understanding Divine Justice

It begins by defining divine justice as depicted in the Scriptures, focusing on its implications for both the righteous and the unrighteous. For example, focus on key biblical passages that describe how God's justice is applied uniformly, such as Romans 2:6, which states, "God will repay each person according to what they have done." This sets the foundation for understanding that divine justice is not merely punitive but fundamentally restorative.

The Mercy of God in Judgment

Contrast the sternness of divine justice with the mercy of God, which offers salvation to all who repent and believe in Jesus Christ. Consider how divine mercy does not negate justice but fulfills it through Christ's atoning sacrifice, referencing 1 John 2:2, "He is the atoning sacrifice for our sins, and not only for ours but also for the sins of the whole world."

―――――――――

Alexandra's Journey to Merge Divine Justice with Human Law

Sarah, a 53-year-old judge, has spent her career navigating the complexities of law and justice. Known for her fairness and wisdom, she carries a small Bible in her briefcase, a grounding presence that guides her through the trials of the courtroom. At the heart of her judicial philosophy is a struggle to balance human justice with divine principles.

Despite her confident exterior, Alexandra wrestles with the harsh realities of the justice system, questioning how her role aligns with the divine justice of God. She grapples with the tension between the need for punishment and the possibility of redemption, particularly in cases where the outcomes seem neither fully just nor merciful.

The pivotal moment for Alexandra occurred during a sentencing hearing for a young man accused of a serious crime. As she prepared to deliver her judgment, she reflected on Romans 2:6 and the universal application of God's justice. Her heart weighed heavy with the responsibility, recognizing her decision's lasting impact on the young man's life.

Moved by a deep sense of compassion and driven by her understanding of divine justice, Alexandra decided to incorporate a restorative justice approach into the sentencing. She recommended not only a penal consequence but also a rehabilitation program designed to provide the young man an opportunity for redemption and transformation.

Alexandra's decision sparked significant discussions within her community and among her peers about the role of mercy within the framework of justice. Her story illustrates the challenging interplay between human judgment and divine justice, highlighting how mercy can complement justice without compromising it.

Through her actions, Alexandra embodies the principle that divine justice, while absolute, includes mercy as a core aspect. She becomes a conduit for showing how earthly decisions can reflect heavenly values, influencing both the lives she touches directly and the broader justice system. Her journey encourages others to consider how they, too, can apply the concepts of divine justice and mercy in their own spheres of influence, promoting a justice that restores rather than only punishes.

Living in the Light of Eternity

This section aims to inspire readers to live each day with the awareness of eternity's imminent reality, emphasizing how this perspective should fundamentally alter our priorities, relationships, and spiritual commitments.

Daily Decisions in Eternal Perspective

Explore practical ways to integrate an eternal perspective into daily decision-making processes. Encourage yourself to evaluate your choices, big and small, through the lens of eternity—asking whether your actions contribute to or detract from your eternal legacy.

Building Eternal Relationships

Focus on relationships and how they should be influenced by our understanding of eternity. Consider how the command to love one another gains even greater significance when viewed against the backdrop of forever, using Scriptures like 1 Peter 4:8, "Above all, love each other deeply, because love covers over a multitude of sins."

Cultivating Spiritual Vigilance

Finally, call yourself to a heightened spiritual vigilance, urging yourself to remain watchful and prepared, much like the wise virgins in the parable of the ten virgins (Matthew 25:1–13). Emphasize the importance of nurturing a vibrant and active faith that is ready to respond whenever the Master calls.

THE FINAL JUDGMENT

Isaac's Guide to Investing in Eternity

Isaac, a 45-year-old financial advisor, meticulously plans for futures—both his clients' and his own. Known for his strategic thinking, he wears a watch gifted by his late father, reminding him that time, although measurable, is infinitely valuable. While adept at securing financial legacies, Isaac seeks to align his life more closely with eternal values.

Amidst the hustle of financial forecasts and investment strategies, Isaac often feels a disconnect between his professional success and his spiritual fulfillment. He questions whether his daily efforts are building something that will last beyond his lifetime or merely fleeting gains.

The turning point for Isaac came during an annual review meeting with a long-time client, where discussions about retirement plans subtly shifted to reflections on life's deeper meanings and legacies. Inspired by the conversation, Isaac realized that his expertise in financial planning could also be a tool for teaching others about the importance of living with an eternal perspective.

Motivated by this new insight, Isaac began integrating questions of eternal value into his consultations, encouraging his clients to consider not just financial security, but also the legacy they wished to leave behind. He started workshops titled "Investing in Eternity," where financial planning met spiritual introspection, guiding clients to align their wealth with their values.

Through his professional platform, Isaac fosters a community where decisions are made with eternity in mind. He emphasizes building relationships that transcend transactions and nurtures a culture of spiritual vigilance among his clients and colleagues.

Encouraged by the impact of his workshops, Isaac deepens his own spiritual practices, engaging more actively in his church and community, embodying the principle that true preparedness for eternity begins with how we live today. His story exemplifies that living in the light of eternity not only enriches our spiritual lives but also enhances our daily interactions and long-term planning, creating a legacy that resonates beyond the bounds of time.

═══════

Conclusion

As we draw chapter ten, "The Final Judgement," to a close, we stand at a pivotal point in our journey through "Faith On Trial." This chapter has led us through a profound exploration of the realities of eternity, the final judgment, and the lasting impact of our earthly lives.

We began by confronting "The Final Verdict: The Christian's Stand Before God," a moment that encapsulates the culmination of our faith journey. This exploration has reminded us that every action, every word, and every decision we make carries weight in the light of eternity. It's a sobering yet inspiring realization that calls us to live with intention and accountability.

In "Eternity's Echo: The Lasting Impact of Our Earthly Journey," we reflected on how our lives resonate beyond our temporal existence. This segment has encouraged us to view our daily choices through the lens of eternity, understanding that our legacy is not just what we leave behind but what we send ahead.

As we conclude this chapter, we are reminded of the call to live purposefully and faithfully, with an eye towards eternity. Let this understanding shape our priorities, guide our actions, and influence our interactions. May we strive to be individuals whose lives reflect the values and teachings of Christ, leaving an indelible mark that echoes into eternity.

This chapter has been a journey of preparation—preparing our hearts, minds, and souls for the eternal realities that await us. It's a reminder to cherish each moment, to live in alignment with God's will, and to make the most of the time we have been given.

In closing chapter ten, "The Final Judgement," let us carry with us the lessons learned about the eternal significance of our earthly journey. May this chapter serve as a guiding light, leading us to live in a way that honors God and resonates with His eternal truth and love.

FAITH ON TRIAL

Afterword

Where Do We Go from Here?

As we close the pages of "Faith On Trial: The Startling Reality of Genuine Belief," we find ourselves at the end of profound journey. This exploration through the ten chapters has been more than an intellectual exercise; it has been a spiritual odyssey. We've delved into the depths of what it means to have genuine faith, confronted challenging truths, and emerged with a deeper understanding of our spiritual convictions.

Throughout this journey, we have navigated the complexities of belief and doubt, the intricacies of faith and false assurance, and the profound realities of salvation and eternity. Each chapter has invited us to reflect, question, and to grow.

As you, the reader, stand at this juncture, my hope is that this book has not only enlightened your mind but also touched your heart. The trials of faith are not mere hurdles; they are opportunities for growth, transformation, and deeper communion with the divine.

Where Do We Go from Here?

Looking ahead, the journey does not end here. "Faith On Trial" is just the beginning, the first drop in the vast ocean of The Living Waters Series. We are on a path of continuous exploration, and the waters of spiritual understanding are deep and wide.

The prequel, "Passion for Christ: New Beginnings," laid the foundation; and now, as we move to book two, "Drenched in Faith: The Transformative Act of Water Baptism," we prepare to dive deeper into the symbolic and transformative journey of baptism. This next book will explore how this sacred act is not just a ritual but a profound expression of faith, a public declaration of a private commitment, and a transformative step in the Christian journey.

In "Drenched in Faith," we will explore the historical, biblical, and spiritual significance of water baptism. We will delve into personal testimonies, scriptural insights, and theological interpretations to understand how this act serves as a pivotal moment in the believer's life.

AFTERWORD

As we journey through The Living Waters Series, each book is designed to take you deeper into the mysteries and joys of the Christian faith. We will explore themes of grace, discipleship, spiritual warfare, the Holy Spirit, and the church's role in the modern world.

Your journey through "Faith On Trial" is a stepping stone to a greater understanding and a deeper relationship with God. As you continue with "Drenched in Faith," and the subsequent books in The Living Waters Series, may your heart be open, your faith strengthened, and your spirit refreshed by the living waters of God's truth.

May this series be a source of inspiration, guidance, and transformative insights as you continue your journey in faith.

God bless . . .

Lori Ann Moeszinger

Bibliography

The Living Waters Series

In the quest to explore the depths of what it truly means to be a follower of Christ, the journey often leads us to the wisdom of many who have walked the path before us. "Passion for Christ: New Beginnings," along with its ten resulting volumes in The Living Waters Series, and then, "In sacred Conversation: The New Testament Prayer Guide" stands as a beacon, illuminating the various facets of Christian living.

The bibliography presented herein is not merely a list; it is a tapestry woven from the threads of countless believers, theologians, historians, and spiritual leaders whose insights and experiences have been invaluable in shaping the discourse within these pages. It serves as an atlas, guiding the earnest seeker through the landscapes of thought that have been traversed to bring these works to fruition.

Each book has been carefully selected to enrich understanding, to challenge preconceptions, and to offer solace and strength on this pilgrimage we embark upon in our daily lives. They are not just citations but conversations with the past, dialogues with the divine, and intersections with ideas that compel us towards a deeper, more profound faith.

As you peruse this bibliography, may it be more than a reference. May it become a repository of knowledge, a companion in study, and gateway to an ever-expanding world of theological richness and spiritual depth. Here lies the foundation upon which The Living Waters Series is built— each book contributing to the symphony of voices that call us to live out faith with vigor and sincerity.

May this bibliography serve you as your guide and inspiration, beckoning you to further exploration, deeper understanding, and a more passionate pursuit of the One who calls us to new beginnings.

The Living Waters Series

The Living Waters Series is a beacon for all those navigating the depths of Christian faith. Encompassing a collection of twelve transformative works, including the cornerstone overview, "Passion for Christ: New Beginnings," this series is a comprehensive journey through the core tenets of Christianity. From the awakening of the soul to the embrace of eternity, each book delves into critical aspects of belief, practice, and divine experience. Readers are offered a wellspring of wisdom on salvation, baptism, filled with the

Holy Spirit, Scripture, church community, tithing, giving, praying for unsaved loved ones, evangelism, and living a life that echoes beyond time. Crafted for both new believers and seasoned disciples, The Living Waters Series stands as a testament to the enduring power of faith and the relentless love of God that flows through every page.

Passion for Christ: New Beginning

Moeszinger, Lori Ann. Passion for Christ: New Beginnings. The Ridge Publishing Group, August 2024.

In her poignant and insightful book, "Passion for Christ: New Beginnings," Lori Ann Moeszinger embarks on an in-depth exploration of transformative Christian living, providing a vital resource for both new converts and long-standing believers seeking to renew their faith. As the first installment of The Living Waters Series, this volume not only introduces readers to the fundamental principles of living a Christ-centered life but also guides them through the practical aspects of incorporating these principles into daily activities and decisions.

Moeszinger adeptly combines theological depth with accessible writing to address the challenges of maintaining spiritual integrity in the modern world. With each chapter, she carefully unpacks the virtues of a life surrendered to Christ, using scriptural references and personal anecdotes to enhance the reader's understanding and application of biblical teachings. This book is an essential guide for anyone committed to pursuing a deep, authentic relationship with God through Jesus Christ, promising not just spiritual insights but a transformative journey of the heart and soul.

Faith On Trial:
The Startling Reality of Genuine Belief

Moeszinger, Lori Ann. Faith On Trial: The Startling Reality of Genuine Belief. The Living Waters Series. The Ridge Publishing Group, September 2024.

Lori Ann Moeszinger's "Faith On Trial: The Startling Reality of Genuine Belief" serves as the opening volume of The Living Waters Series, inviting readers into a compelling journey through the depths of authentic Christian faith. This book confronts essential questions about the nature of belief, the essence of grace, and the rigor of salvation with an unflinching clarity that is both challenging and enlightening.

Structured around critical examinations of foundational Christian doctrines—such as the Roman Road and the Four Spiritual Laws—"Faith On Trial" offers readers a rigorous pathway to assess and affirm the authenticity of their faith. Through thoughtful analysis and personal introspection, Moeszinger encourages believers to scrutinize their spiritual convictions against biblical standards, providing a comprehensive guide to understanding and embracing a genuine Christian life.

Each chapter in "Faith On Trial" is designed not only to inform but to transform, urging readers to consider deeply the eternal implications of their faith and their readiness to stand before God. This book is a must-read for anyone seeking to deepen their spiritual understanding and to live out a faith that truly withstands the trials and tribulations of modern life.

Drenched in Faith:
The Transformative Act of Water Baptism

Moeszinger, Lori Ann. Drenched in Faith: The Transformative Act of Water Baptism. The Living Waters Series. The Ridge Publishing Group, October 2024.

In the second installment of The Living Waters Series, Lori Ann Moeszinger offers a profound exploration into the spiritual significance of baptism in "Drenched in Faith: The Transformative Act of Water Baptism." This book navigates through the historical, symbolic, and deeply personal aspects of baptism, presenting it as a crucial rite of passage for believers.

Moeszinger delves into the roots of baptism from its biblical origins to its modern-day applications, exploring how this ancient ritual acts as a bridge between personal faith and communal identity. The book provides a thorough investigation into whether baptism is merely a symbolic act or a necessary step towards salvation, examining its role in shaping Christian identity across the ages.

Each chapter of "Drenched in Faith" is designed to engage readers with theological insights and spiritual reflections, encouraging them to consider how baptism's transformative power can impact their own lives and the lives of those around them. From the cleansing waters of the Jordan River to the sacred spaces of contemporary churches, Moeszinger invites readers to rediscover baptism as a dynamic and ongoing act of faith that continues to resonate with profound spiritual significance.

This book is essential for anyone seeking to deepen their understanding of a foundational Christian practice. It challenges believers to rethink the role of baptism within the broader context of their spiritual journey, making it a vital resource for those looking to embrace a life truly drenched in faith.

Spirit Filled Life:
The Unseen Force of Divine Power

Moeszinger, Lori Ann. Spirit Filled Life: The Unseen Force of Divine Power. The Living Waters Series. The Ridge Publishing Group, November 2024.

In the third installment of The Living Waters Series, Lori Ann Moeszinger takes readers on a profound journey into the supernatural realms of Christianity in "Spirit Filled Life: The Unseen Force of Divine Power." This book provides a comprehensive exploration of the Holy Spirit's dynamic role in the believer's life, from the dramatic events of Pentecost to the subtle guidances in daily living.

Moeszinger offers deep biblical insights, historical contexts, and personal testimonies to illustrate the transformative impact of being filled with the Holy Spirit. The book discusses various manifestations of the Holy Spirit, such as speaking in tongues and prophetic insights, and distinguishes between public expressions of faith and intimate spiritual experiences.

Each chapter is designed not only to inform but also to inspire and challenge readers to invite the Holy Spirit more fully into their lives. Moeszinger encourages a deeper engagement with the Spirit's power, promising readers a renewed sense of faith and a more profound understanding of God's presence.

"Spirit Filled Life" serves as both a theological guide and a practical manual for those seeking to enhance their spiritual journey through Holy Spirit empowerment. It is an essential resource for anyone wishing to explore the breadth and depth of the Spirit's work in their life and to experience the full potential of living a Spirit-empowered life.

The Bible Unbound:
Trust, Translation, and Transformation

Moeszinger, Lori Ann. The Bible Unbound: Trust, Translation, and Transformation. The Living Waters Series. The Ridge Publishing Group, December 2024.

In the fourth installment of The Living Waters Series, Lori Ann Moeszinger delivers a compelling exploration of the Bible in "The Bible Unbound: Trust, Translation, and Transformation." This book offers readers an in-depth look into the authenticity of Bible translations, the interpretation of prophecy, and the application of biblical truths to modern life.

Moeszinger expertly guides readers through the complex landscape of Scripture, addressing common misconceptions and highlighting the enduring relevance of the Bible. Through a blend of scholarly research and accessible writing, she explores how accurate translations impact our understanding of ancient texts and unpacks the most enigmatic prophecies with clarity.

Each chapter of "The Bible Unbound" serves as both a lesson in biblical scholarship and a testament to the transformative power of Scripture. Moeszinger encourages readers to delve deeper into their faith by engaging with the Bible in a way that is both informed and passionate. This book is an essential resource for anyone seeking to deepen their understanding of Scripture and its application to their daily lives, providing the tools needed to navigate the rich terrain of biblical teachings and to embrace the Bible's transformative power in personal and communal contexts.

"The Bible Unbound" is more than a guide; it is an invitation to experience the Bible as a living, breathing entity that offers renewal and guidance for believers seeking to align their lives with eternal truths. This work is an indispensable part of any Christian's library, offering profound insights that promise to enrich the reader's spiritual journey and understanding of their faith.

Prophets and Pulpits:
Discerning Truth in the House of God

Moeszinger, Lori Ann. Prophets and Pulpits: Discerning Truth in the House of God. The Living Waters Series. The Ridge Publishing Group, January 2025.

In the fifth volume of The Living Waters Series, Lori Ann Moeszinger delivers a probing examination of modern church practices and prophetic claims in "Prophets and Pulpits: Discerning Truth in the House of God." This book challenges believers to cultivate a discerning spirit towards spiritual leadership and worship, encouraging a return to Scripture-based truth and authenticity.

Moeszinger navigates through the intricate landscape of contemporary Christian worship, offering a critical look at how cultural customs intersect with and often obscure biblical doctrines. The book addresses hot-button issues such as the validity of modern prophetic voices, the authenticity of church practices, and the origins of commonly accepted Christian holidays like Christmas, providing a balanced perspective rooted in solid theological research.

"Prophets and Pulpits" serves not only as an educational resource but also as a guide for personal and communal spiritual growth. Moeszinger equips readers with the tools necessary to discern genuine biblical teachings from prevalent myths, promoting a deeper understanding of what it means to engage in genuine worship and follow godly leadership.

The book is a vital resource for anyone seeking to deepen their knowledge of church doctrine and enhance their worship experience. It is particularly useful for those wishing to understand the nuances of prophetic claims and the dynamics of spiritual authority within the context of modern Christianity.

Through engaging narrative and rigorous analysis, "Prophets and Pulpits" offers a transformative look at the essentials of a robust Christian faith, making it an indispensable addition to any believer's library who is eager to ensure their faith practices are grounded in truth and aligned with the teachings of Scripture.

Beyond the Tithe:
The Transformative Power of Generous Faith

Moeszinger, Lori Ann. Beyond the Tithe: The Transformative Power of Generous Faith. The Living Waters Series. The Ridge Publishing Group, February 2025.

In the sixth installment of The Living Waters Series, Lori Ann Moeszinger takes readers on a profound journey in "Beyond the Tithe: The Transformative Power of Generous Faith," exploring the spiritual richness that emerges from transcending traditional tithing practices. This volume challenges and encourages readers to redefine their understanding of generosity and its profound impact on both the giver and the receiver.

Delving into the biblical foundations of giving and its implications for modern believers, Moeszinger expertly weaves together scriptural insights, personal stories, and theological reflections to illustrate how generosity extends far beyond monetary contributions. She explores the joy and spiritual growth that come from a life characterized by giving, urging readers to embrace a more expansive view of generosity as a core element of Christian faith.

"Beyond the Tithe" not only discusses the historical and biblical context of tithing but also encourages a deeper, more intentional practice of generosity. Through compelling narrative and actionable advice, Moeszinger inspires readers to integrate generosity into their daily lives as a means of fostering spiritual development and enriching their communities.

This book serves as an essential guide for anyone seeking to deepen their spiritual journey through the practice of generous living. It is an invaluable resource for understanding how the act of giving can transform lives, build lasting legacies, and reflect the love of Christ in tangible ways.

Join Lori Ann Moeszinger in discovering the transformative power of generosity and learn how expanding your practice of giving can lead to a richer, more fulfilling faith journey.

Heart of Abundance:
The Journey to Radical Giving and Receiving

Moeszinger, Lori Ann. Heart of Abundance: The Journey to Radical Giving and Receiving. The Living Waters Series. The Ridge Publishing Group, March 2025.

In the seventh book of The Living Waters Series, Lori Ann Moeszinger leads readers into the enriching world of generosity in "Heart of Abundance: The Journey to Radical Giving and Receiving." This volume delves into the transformative power of generosity, exploring how radical giving and receiving can fundamentally enrich one's life and spirit.

Moeszinger expertly combines compelling narratives with profound biblical insights, illustrating how the acts of giving and receiving are not just transactions but transformative experiences that reflect divine love and foster deep personal fulfillment. Through stories of individuals and communities engaging in acts of unprecedented generosity, the book inspires readers to open their hearts and extend their hands in ways that leave lasting impacts.

"Heart of Abundance" challenges its readers to rethink traditional perceptions of generosity and to embrace a lifestyle of abundant giving that aligns with biblical teachings. It encourages a holistic view of generosity that transcends mere material giving and receives, promoting a life enriched by spiritual depth and communal connection.

This book is an essential resource for anyone seeking to deepen their understanding of spiritual abundance and to practice generosity in transformative ways. It provides practical guidance and inspiring examples that equip readers to start their own journey of radical generosity, aiming to cultivate a legacy of love and purpose that resonates through their lives and beyond.

Join Lori Ann Moeszinger in "Heart of Abundance" to discover how embracing radical generosity can lead you to a life filled with joy, purpose, and abundant fulfillment.

Heaven's Reach:
Drawing the Unbelieving into the Fold

Moeszinger, Lori Ann. Heaven's Reach: Drawing the Unbelieving into the Fold. The Living Waters Series. The Ridge Publishing Group, April 2025.

In the eighth book of The Living Waters Series, Lori Ann Moeszinger tackles the profound power of intercessory prayer in "Heaven's Reach: Drawing the Unbelieving into the Fold." This volume delves into the spiritual practice of interceding for those who have not yet embraced faith, exploring the transformative impact such prayers can have on both the individual and the wider community.

Moeszinger expertly combines theological insights with practical advice, providing readers with a comprehensive guide to intercessory prayer. Through compelling stories and a deep biblical understanding, she illustrates how strategic and compassionate prayer can bridge the gap between skepticism and faith, transforming doubts into devotion and indifference into fervor.

"Heaven's Reach" is designed to empower readers to cultivate a deeper compassion for the unbelieving and to engage in the mission of evangelism through prayer. The book is a call to action, encouraging believers to take up the mantle of intercessors, fostering a legacy of faith that reaches beyond personal boundaries and into the hearts of those around them.

This installment is an essential resource for anyone looking to deepen their understanding of evangelistic prayer and its role in drawing the unbelieving into a life of faith. It offers not just knowledge, but also the tools needed for readers to become active participants in what Moeszinger describes as "the greatest commission given to mankind."

Join Lori Ann Moeszinger in "Heaven's Reach" to discover the profound joy and fulfillment that comes from engaging in the transformative power of prayer and witness the change it can bring to the world.

Breaking Silence:
The Charge to Uphold the Faith Out Loud

Moeszinger, Lori Ann. Breaking Silence: The Charge to Uphold the Faith Out Loud. The Living Waters Series. The Ridge Publishing Group, May 2025.

In the ninth book of The Living Waters Series, Lori Ann Moeszinger delivers a compelling call to action with "Breaking Silence: The Charge to Uphold the Faith Out Loud." This installment challenges believers to vocalize their faith boldly and effectively, transforming them from silent observers to vocal advocates for Christ in a world desperate for truth.

Through a blend of scriptural wisdom and actionable advice, Moeszinger equips readers to navigate the complexities of modern evangelism. She tackles the barriers that often keep Christians silent, offering strategies to overcome fear and resistance while encouraging a dynamic expression of faith that resonates in both personal interactions and broader societal engagement.

"Breaking Silence" serves as both a guide and an inspiration for Christians eager to make their faith audible in the cacophony of global discourse. It provides practical steps for engaging in vocal faith advocacy, emphasizing the importance of truth spoken with love and conviction. Moeszinger's insightful guidance helps readers harness the power of their voice to bridge gaps, heal divisions, and lead others toward the transformative power of the Gospel.

This book is an essential tool for anyone ready to take their faith expression to the next level, offering both the why and the how of effective communication. Prepare to be inspired, challenged, and equipped to make your faith heard in a world yearning for hope and direction.

Join Lori Ann Moeszinger in a movement that not only breaks the silence but also builds a legacy of faith that echoes through eternity.

Beyond the Final Breath:
The Christian's Voyage into Eternity

Moeszinger, Lori Ann. *Beyond the Final Breath: The Christian's Voyage into Eternity*. The Living Waters Series. The Ridge Publishing Group, June 2025.

In the monumental finale of The Living Waters Series, Lori Ann Moeszinger provides readers with a profound exploration into the Christian perspective on life after death in "Beyond the Final Breath: The Christian's Voyage into Eternity." This book serves as a spiritual guide, offering deep biblical insights and thoughtful inquiries into the mysteries of the afterlife and the soul's journey beyond mortal existence.

Through a blend of scriptural interpretation and reflective exploration, Moeszinger challenges readers to consider the profound questions surrounding our eternal destiny. She navigates through complex theological terrain with clarity and compassion, addressing topics such as the nature of the eternal body, the significance of the Lamb's Book of Life, and what Scripture reveals about the afterlife.

"Beyond the Final Breath" is crafted not only to inform but also to inspire readers to align their earthly lives with God's eternal promises. It encourages a life that views its conclusion not as an end but as the commencement of a glorious, eternal existence. This book is an indispensable resource for anyone seeking to understand the biblical teachings on eternity and how they apply to personal faith and the broader Christian hope.

Join Lori Ann Moeszinger in this culminating volume as she guides you through the Christian eternal journey, preparing you for a life beyond death filled with hope and glory. This is more than just a book—it is a beacon for all who seek to live their earthly lives in anticipation of their eternal home.

In Sacred Conversation: Getting Your Prayer Life In Order

Moeszinger, Lori Ann. In Sacred Conversation: Getting Your Prayer Life In Order. The Living Waters Series Sequel. The Ridge Publishing Group, July 2025.

As a sequel to the widely acclaimed The Living Waters Series, Lori Ann Moeszinger's "In Sacred Conversation: Getting Your Prayer Life In Order" offers readers an insightful and practical guide to mastering the art of prayer according to New Testament principles. This book explores ten fundamental prayers, elucidating their significance and application in the daily lives of believers, aiming to deepen their communion with God.

The guide is meticulously structured to enhance the reader's understanding of effective prayer, incorporating scriptural foundations and practical steps to develop a disciplined prayer routine. Moeszinger integrates biblical insights with contemporary relevance, making each lesson accessible and actionable for modern Christians seeking to fortify their prayer lives.

"In Sacred Conversation" is designed not only to educate but also to transform, encouraging readers to integrate prayer seamlessly into their daily routine, thus enriching their spiritual journey and relationship with God. It serves as an essential resource for anyone eager to enhance their communication with the divine, providing the tools needed for a more profound, effective spiritual practice.

This sequel continues the tradition of The Living Waters Series by guiding readers through a detailed exploration of biblical teachings, encouraging them to live out their faith with confidence and sincerity. Ideal for both new and seasoned believers, "In Sacred Conversation" is more than just a book—it's a spiritual mentor for all who seek to align their prayer life with God's eternal promises.

FAITH ON TRIAL

Author Photo © 2023 Edwin Wolfe

LORI ANN MOESZINGER, affectionately known as "L," stands at the creative helm of The Ridge Publishing Group and its diverse imprints. A prolific American author, insightful blogger, and dynamic publisher, she crafts words that resonate and narratives that captivate. Now, nestled in the scenic tranquility of Coeur d'Alene, Idaho, Lori finds inspiration in the lakeside whispers and the companionship of her husband and their two beloved dogs.

Her writing journey traverses various pseudonyms, each a distinct facet of her expansive expertise. As Ann Patterson, she delves into the intricacies of business law, distilling complex concepts into clear, actionable advice. Under the byline L. A. Moeszinger, she navigates the nuanced realms of writing, marketing, and publishing, guiding aspiring authors toward their dreams. In her biblical and personal writings, she embraces her full name, Lori Ann Moeszinger, offering reflections steeped in faith and introspection.

Yet, it's through the New Youniversity Chronicles, The Manhattan Diaries series that Lori's versatility truly shines, showcasing her storytelling prowess across a spectrum of voices, each as engaging and unique as the last. Her foundational belief in faith's power, the virtue of blessings, and the virtues of industrious dedication pulses through every line she writes.

Transcending her former life as a lawyer, Lori now revels in the freedom of expression that authorship and publishing afford—a stark contrast to the rigid confines of law. Her new chapter is one marked by a fervent passion for empowering others, a commitment to hard work, and the joy of sharing her literary gifts.

Discover the multifaced worlds Lori has woven at her websites and blog sites, or connect with her on her social media platforms where she continues to inspire, educate, and transform the written word into a shared experience of growth and discovery.

Parent Website: https://www.RidgePublishingGroup.com and

blog site https://www.PublisherAndHerWorld.com

Publisher Website: https://www.GuardiansofBiblicalTruth.com and

blog site https://www.Jesus-Says.com

Author website: https://www.LAMoeszinger.com and New Youniversity sites:

https://www.NewYouniversity.com, https://www.ManhattanChronicles.com

Bridge Website: https://www.AuthorsDoor.com and

blog site https://www.AuthorsRedDoor.com

Entertainment website: https://www.EthanFoxBooks.com and

blog site https://www.KidsStagram.com

Want More?

Welcome to Coffee with God! Jesus-Says.com! Dive into our blog for inspiring insights and biblical truths that deepen your faith and enrich your spiritual journey. Explore thought-provoking articles, personal testimonies, and practical guidance rooted in Scripture. Whether you're new to the faith or a lifelong believer, Jesus-Says offers wisdom and encouragement for your walk with Christ. Join our community and grow in your relationship with God!

Guardians of Biblical Truth Hub

Welcome to our Guardians of Biblical Truth Facebook page! Join our community to deepen your understanding of the Bible and live out its principles. Engage in enriching Bible studies, share faith testimonies, and connect with like-minded believers. Whether you're new to the faith or a seasoned believer, you'll find support and inspiration here. Join us today and grow in your walk with Christ.

Guardians of Biblical Truth Forum

Welcome to our Guardians of Biblical Truth Forum! Join our closed Facebook group to deepen your understanding of the Bible and strengthen your faith. Engage in enriching discussions, share personal testimonies, and connect with a supportive community of believers. Whether you're new to the faith or a seasoned believer, you'll find inspiration and encouragement here. Join us today and grow in your walk with Christ!

_____

_____